Back There Where the Past Was

Back There

Where the Past Was

A Small-Town Boyhood

CHARLES CHAMPLIN
Foreword by RAY BRADBURY

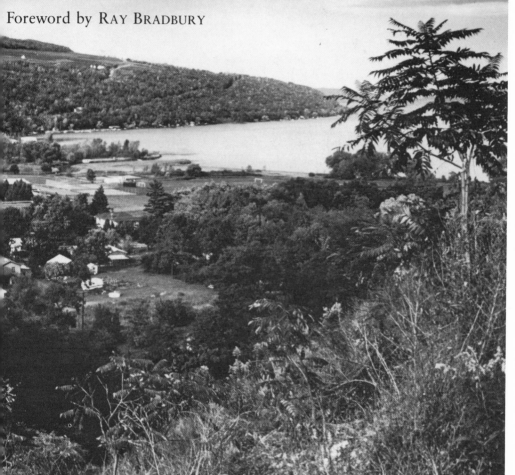

SYRACUSE UNIVERSITY PRESS

First Edition, 1989
99 98 97 96 95 94 93 92 91 90 89   6 5 4 3 2

This book has been published with the assistance of a grant from the John Ben Snow Foundation.

The paper used in this publication meets the minimum requirements of American National Standard for Information Sciences—Permanence of Paper for Printed Library Materials, ANSI Z39.48-1984. ∞™

Library of Congress Cataloging-in-Publication Data

Champlin, Charles, 1926–
    Back there where the past was: a small-town boyhood/Charles Champlin.—1st ed.
        p. cm.—(York State book)
    Bibliography: p.
    ISBN 0-8156-0235-9 (alk. paper)
    1. Champlin, Charles, 1926– —Childhood and youth.
    2. Hammondsport (N.Y.)—Biography. 3. Hammondsport (N.Y.)—Social life and customs. 4. City and town life—New York (State)—
—Hammondsport. I. Title.
    F129.H24C48 1989
    974.7'83—dc19
    [B]   88-38643
                                                                           CIP

MANUFACTURED IN THE UNITED STATES OF AMERICA

On the title page: A view of Hammondsport looking west. The town is almost hidden by its ancient maples. There are vineyards on the far hills. Keuka Lake stretches north twenty-two miles to Penn Yan.

Unless otherwise noted, photographs are by the author or from his collection.

This is for Peggy
with love and thanks

CHARLES CHAMPLIN has been a working journalist since he graduated from Harvard College in 1948 after serving two years in the Infantry in World War II. From 1948 to 1965 he was a reporter, correspondent, and writer for *Life* and *Time* magazines in New York, Chicago, Denver, Los Angeles, and London. He has been the arts editor and a columnist for the *Los Angeles Times* since 1965 and was also the newspaper's principal film critic between 1967 and 1980. He met his wife in the Hammondsport Public Library and married her in St. Gabriel's Church. They have six children and five grandchildren.

Contents

Illustrations

Foreword

I think that by now most of us have given enough thought to disagree with Thomas Wolfe's novelized assertion, *You Can't Go Home Again.*

You can indeed. But we go on separate paths and in different ways.

Dreaming at night, we go home. Walking by day we see a certain autumn-bright tree, and our birthplace returns.

Or, truly going home, we arrive with glorious luck late on some autumn afternoon when the sunset burnishes each and every thing to brass and copper. When every cupola is gold and ten thousand windows lift like warrior's shields, all burning bright.

If we are smart, we leave in the same weather, at early morn when the sun in the opposite sky sets wildfires to ignite the town.

Sherwood Anderson, of course, went home to find streets mobbed with gargoyles somehow fallen off a pintsize local Notre Dame and thriving on the outhouses and porches of Winesburg, Ohio.

Stephen Leacock, in one of his most hilarious and touching pedestrian-and-paddlewheel excursions made landfall with the Missewappi Belle to harvest timberlands of cliche with his hyperbolic wit as his bid for immortality with *Sunshine Sketches of a Little Town.*

Steinbeck hardly left home. He trapped Salinas and its high

grey fogs, Hispanic laborers, and the Cannery Row just beyond the high hills, forever.

The list is endless.

Charles Champlin is only one in a chain of young men who ran away in reality or ran off in their minds, only to find that Time Indeed Had Stopped waiting for their return, or Time did a quick fast-forward leaving them behind forever.

What about Charles Champlin, now?

He is a kind man, willing to peel off at least one layer of his outer skin so as to perceive with his entire self these encounters, surprised here.

Yet, sensitive dermis and all, he does not let the homecoming surprises knock him bum over brains into sentimentality.

All of the weathercocks on all of his rediscovered rooftops spin and settle toward honest sentiment which is the hardest weather to describe and the most difficult direction to track for most writers.

Which means that I open this book to read with perfect trust.

Trust in what? Total or almost total recall. Play that along with intuitive recognition, as Charles Champlin strolls back and forth in time, and an impulse for the Aside, and you have a first-rate writer.

For if a writer is not 98 percent intuition and two percent humidity under the arms, he is nothing. Champlin has perfected not only striking targets head-on, but leans toward that best art, that of digression, *not* brevity, that is the soul of wit. For me, anyway.

We go to *Hamlet, Othello* and *Richard III* for that grand release: digression. We don't give a hoot in hell who poisoned the King of Denmark's semicircular canal. We already know where Desdemona lies smothered in bedclothes and that Richard goes headless at his finale. We attend them to toss pebbles in ponds, not to see the stones strike, but the ripples spread.

Digression works upon the philosophical mysteries of life, which attract us with their insolubility.

Chuck Champlin has written just such a book. It would be nothing if it were all bullseye and no echoing concentric rings. There are plenty of echoes, plenty of spreading ripples here as you will find band concert nights full of mosquitoes, crickets and brass, skies full of still primitive parachute-birthing planes, garages from which our wild early-on American technologies were born, hard times in which we didn't know we were poor because our family never told us, and school teachers we fell in love with (the same teacher, cloned, in every town in every year in all of our lives).

I went back, much as Chuck Champlin did, to my grandparents' house some eight years ago, walked up on the lawn and picked a dandelion. An old woman came out of the house and called down to me, "If I see a stranger picking a dandelion on my lawn, it has to be Ray Bradbury. Come in."

Similarly if someone in Hammondsport saw a somewhat familiar stranger wandering its streets with a quietly amiable face and brightly curious but not intrusive eyes, his hands in his pockets, *not* taking notes, but drinking everything in and not only drinking it in but remembering, yes, remembering it, he would have to say:

"Why, hell, that's *got* to be Chuck Champlin. Remember him, Ma? That nice kid who could easily have been a priest but became a fine writer, and remembered more than we had all forgot."

That says it.

I now stand aside to let Hammondsport in the Thirties, let Charles Champlin on his long quiet easy perambulation, happen.

Los Angeles, California   RAY BRADBURY
October 18, 1988

Preface

As someone who has reported the Academy Awards for years I know how numbingly dull the endless litanies of the thankful are. But in a real sense not even an autobiographical book writes itself; writers no less than actors need support systems and are grateful for them.

Accordingly I am grateful to a succession of editors at the *Los Angeles Times,* who have tolerated the appearance of undated essays amid the urgencies of daily journalism. Jean Sharley Taylor, Nick Williams, Bill Thomas, Jim Bellows and the late Leonard Riblett provided the tolerant environment in which the idea of this book took shape.

I owe great thanks to my brother Monsignor Joseph Champlin and my cousins Caroline Champlin Chamberlain and W. E. (Tony) Doherty who reviewed the manuscript for signs of a shaky memory (all surviving errors being mine alone). For close readings and insightful comments on the book I am indebted as well to Marilee Zdenek, Diana de Villafranca and Florence Stone.

I am grateful to Lucille Robinson of the Hammondsport Public Library for information on the early days of the village and to the Glenn H. Curtiss Museum of Local History for making available material on the Glenn Curtiss years, and for permission to use photographs from their collection.

I owe particularly thanks to my patient agent and encouraging friend for these many years, Ned Brown.

The dedication speaks for itself but I must add specifically that the proofreading and the checking by my wife Peggy, as well as her encouragement, have been invaluable. This book is, not least, a partial answer to years of questions from our children (Chuck, Katy, John, Judi, Susan, and Nancy) about what it was like to grow up in Hammondsport, and I'm glad they asked.

I give great thanks, finally, to six decades' worth of Hammondsport friends and neighbors who were contributing to this book without knowing it, and to the many readers of the *Los Angeles Times* who persuaded me that Hammondsport was larger than Hammondsport—an emblem of life in a great many communities in the middle American thirties and forties.

Los Angeles, California, and   CHARLES CHAMPLIN
Hammondsport, New York
October, 1988

Back There Where the Past Was

Introduction

We are all from somewhere else: some other time and, more than likely in our transient society, from some other place. And I think we never quite lose that sense of being *from*, however much we may come to feel that we belong to whatever place we've got to.

I haven't lived in Hammondsport since 1942, but I have gone back as often as I could over the years, because no other place has ever felt so completely like home to me. Even now, forty-odd years later and against all but the heart's logic, I think of myself as being on a kind of temporary assignment from Hammondsport to the larger world.

In moments of triumph I wish (as would most of us) that the folks back home could see me now; in times of stress I yearn mightily for the simpler strains of my Hammondsport past (carefully forgetting how complicated and unpleasant some of those strains were). When the world delights me, I would eagerly share the delight with the friends of my ancient summers.

I have no doubt that the years I lived in Hammondsport— there were not many, not a quarter of my life as I write this— did more than anything else to shape me: more than college or travel, work or marriage, discoveries or faith. Willa Cather, looking back over a half-century of fiction, told a reporter, "All my stories have been written with the material that was gathered—

1

no, God save us—not gathered but absorbed—before I was fifteen years old" (O'Brien, p. 1311).

I am a writer of nonfiction for the most part, yet I am certain that I could say the same thing as Cather, and that the experiences of those first sixteen years of mine in Hammondsport have, more than anything else, shaped and shaded everything I've written ever since. All writing is finally autobiographical, criticism most especially, because your standards are born of everything you have read, seen, heard, experienced. Even reportage that is ostensibly as objective as a multiplication table is colored by the "I" we are. But the I keeps changing. As the narrator of Christopher Isherwood's novel, *Down There on a Visit*, says, "There has been no break in the sequence of daily statements that I am I. But *what* I am has refashioned itself throughout the days and years, until now almost all that remains constant is the mere awareness of being conscious" (p. 14).

The I who writes now about Hammondsport is not quite the same I who grew up there more than fifty years ago. A good deal has happened meanwhile to both man and town. Yet it is clear to me that life in Hammondsport in those years from the late twenties to the early forties provided what you might call a series of benchmarks against which I measure, unconsciously as well as consciously, the people, the places, and the happenings of my later worlds. It was a rather particular village, if only in that it made champagne and airplanes. It still makes champagne, although the airplanes have flown on into history. Hammondsport was small enough to have, for a boy growing up, a sense of community that was close to the feeling of an extended family, populated with family friends I called aunt and uncle long after I had come to understand the titles were honorary.

Hammondsport was rural, I suppose, more so then than now, but the wine and the flying gave it, in this century certainly, a cosmopolitan flavor that not many outlying towns its size have had. Alexander Graham Bell, one of the attendants at the birth of flight, was a frequent visitor in the early years of the century

2

when Glenn Hammond Curtiss, a Hammondsport lad, was trying to perfect a flying machine. I discovered in a biography only a few years ago that one of my idols, the legendary cornetist Bix Beiderbecke, spent a few days at Hammondsport in the early twenties, a pause during the first trip to New York by his band, The Wolverines. One year, after the World Series, the manager of the New York Yankees, Joe McCarthy, and his star pitcher, Lefty Gomez, came to town for a little pheasant-hunting. They made an appearance at the high school. Hammondsport may have been remote, but it has never been isolated. It is also a lake town, literally a port in its early days and even into the first two decades of this century, and there have always been summer cottagers to enrich the life of Hammondsport in every sense.

My Hammondsport years were a benchmark time for the country as a whole. The very late twenties were roaring into the stock market crash and the Depression which was only arrested by Pearl Harbor and World War II. Hammondsport's own Depression had a headstart on the national woes. It began in 1919 when the Eighteenth Amendment to the Constitution laid Prohibition on the country. Repeal in 1933 had come before I was aware of much beyond the effort of learning to read, write, and add; yet the glimpses of hard times—none of us escaped them, although some were luckier than others—have remained an influencing memory for me as for everyone of my generation.

The fact is that I am, as I realize more clearly right along, what the Hammondsport years helped me to be. And in moments of intense emotion, from pride to loneliness to the intimations of my own mortality, I am somehow never in New York, Chicago, Denver, London or Los Angeles or any of the other places I have lived. I am back in Hammondsport, at the core of my being, so to speak. And I feel myself to be the adult I am and at the same time the child I was, surrounded by faces long gone and voices long stilled, walking amid the grand old elms that are also dead and the maples that survive. In these moments of unwilled reverie, I am suffused by sudden and unlikely recollections, as of

3

trying to roller skate along the root-heaved sidewalks, or being roused from sleep to go to midnight Mass on bitter-chill Christmas Eves.

I have written about Hammondsport many times in my "Critic at Large" column in the pages of the *Los Angeles Times*, indulging the patience of readers on the far side of the continent who will in the main never have heard of Hammondsport before and will probably never come within a thousand miles of it.

But what has astonished me (and encouraged me to sin again and again) is that the Hammondsport pieces have for twenty years now been drawing more response than almost anything else I've done for the paper—more than the film reviews, the profiles, the tributes to the worthy departed, the commentaries on the events of the moment. Partly, of course, it is that there are so many refugees from colder climates in Southern California, and this includes refugees from those upstate New York winters. I sometimes feel as if half the population of Steuben, Chemung, Yates, and several adjoining counties has adjourned to Los Angeles. I have heard from men who worked at the Curtiss factory in 1915 and played in the town band, or who summered at Branchport or Corning Landing, or who remember the tame bear and the water toboggan at Lakeside. I have been chided for getting wrong the name of the theater in Hornell where I heard Bunny Berigan and his orchestra on Sunday afternoon, March 23, 1942, or for mislocating a movie house I attended in Penn Yan.

But I have heard as well, and probably more often, from those who have no links at all with Hammondsport or Lake Keuka or upstate New York. For them, as they tell me with wonderful eloquence, my Hammondsport evokes *their* somewhere else, their town in Indiana or Nebraska, Iowa or Oregon. Hammondsport's bandstand in the park might have been theirs, the Fourth of July oration sounds quite like the one they heard, Labor Day was the same kind of melancholy punctuation in their young lives.

Even the native Californians, and there are a great many of

4

them, tell me they have found resonances to their own lives in the Hammondsport columns, if only in my attempts to summon a past that was, if not better, then clearer and less muddled.

The late Simone Signoret took as the title of her memoirs the wry comment that *Nostalgia Isn't What It Used to Be*. Someone else has said that the best prescription for a happy childhood is a bad memory. I can't help being sentimental about my Hammondsport past, if only because I have tried to remember how things looked to a child's eye, and in childhood things seem, for that fleeting moment, to be simple, even if it is evident all too soon that they aren't simple and never were. I yearn for the innocence that began to erode when I was four, maybe five, yet I also try to remember Hammondsport as it truly was, an invention not exclusively of Norman Rockwell or Judge Hardy, but not on the other hand a Southern Tier Peyton Place or a case study for Stephen King.

I might daringly argue that, at that, Rockwell and the Andy Hardy movies came a little closer to the truth than the darker visions. Hammondsport had its share of sinners and villains, but evil incarnate was in just as short supply as savings.

In the days I have been writing about there was a kind of umbrella of shared certainties over both Hammondsport and the larger society, a whole set of agreed values of right and wrong, good and bad. The verities spoken of on the Fourth of July were understood to be true.

Marx and Freud had done their work but it had not yet seeped significantly into the larger popular consciousness. Nothing, so far as I could remember, had seriously compromised the role of faith or the solidity of the churches in the community. (As I think back, the local church, even the Catholic Church, was the measure of its resident minister or priest. Despite visitations from foreign missionaries and other church dignitaries from away, as we used to say, the churches were local institutions, part of the extended community family, each deriving something of its local image from the character of the men who preached.)

But increasingly in the years since World War II, our society has become unfixed and mobile, so that we are indeed, so many of us, from somewhere else. Along with the mobility, although not directly related to it, has come an erosion of most of the old certainties. There are holes, sievelike almost, in that umbrella of agreed beliefs. It may be that part of the appeal of the Hammondsport pieces has been that they do recall those more settled and confident days, when even the hard times fitted into the context of the way things were and had always been.

The mobility damaged if it did not destroy the strong sense of continuity that seemed central to the life of Hammondsport. The town is not as long-settled as the New England towns further east, but it dates from about 1794, and there are a handful, anyway, of present citizens who can trace their origins back to the earliest families. I can, too, back to Judge Sam Baker, one of the first settlers in Pleasant Valley, just south of town. Then again I am not a present resident but a loyal expatriate. But growing up I was far from alone in being able to identify great-grandparents and even great-great-grandparents in the pretty Pleasant Valley Cemetery where Sam Baker rests.

That sense of continuity is something I regret having been unable to bequeath to my own children, who have been born in four states and two countries. Yet their own mobility has been a trade-off, and out of it I think they have qualities of self-reliance and independence, begat of necessity, that it took me a while to acquire, having been sheltered (or perhaps propped up) by the weight of family tradition. But continuity—knowing the history of every house, the intertwinings of every family—was part of the Hammondsport experience.

The Depression profoundly shook the confidence of the country as a whole in both the free-enterprise system and the ability of a democratic government to cope with the economic mess the society was in. But the shaking was far more profound and the hard times far harder in the cities than in country towns like

Hammondsport, where there was open land and local crops and even the occasional job.

One of my memories is of city families, from Long Island or New Jersey, with their hard, unfamiliar, nasal accents, who drifted into Hammondsport in the Depression years, drawn by the hope or the vague promise of work, and who usually stayed just long enough for the kids to make friends, and then drifted off again, in pursuit of some new and distant, more westerly hope.

One way and another, Hammondsport survived the Depression with its confidences dented yet largely intact, and when I moved away in the summer of 1942 it was still very much the town in which I had grown up.

I have, as I was saying, gone back to Hammondsport as often as I could in the years since, out of affection for a place that is by any standards a perfect and beautiful site for a vacation, and to renew acquaintances with family and old friends. It was really only by chance (or by the imperatives of a thrice-weekly column deadline) that I began to see Hammondsport as a piece of America that not only measured my life but said a good deal about the way we all were, and are. And that's what I have been writing about.

Newspaper columns inevitably betray their deadline timeliness and so acquire a certain early perishability. (I've often said that writing for a newspaper is like carving your initials on the surface of a lake.) In this book I have rethought, regrouped, and rewritten the columns in the hope of sharper clarity and slower perishability.

Going Home

Voyages into your own past are fraught with peril and suspense, full of small shocks and large surprises and flavored by a slight, irrational resentment that anything has been allowed to change in your absence. Yet, once you have sorted out the jumble of sentimental memories and achieved a reasonable reportorial calm, it becomes clear that things remain unchanged only on Greek urns and in mausoleums. What you are wisest to hope about home is that it has undergone a kind of continuing renewal that honors and retains the best of the past, but is not the captive of it. I haven't liked all the changes I have watched in Hammondsport over the years. As they have in villages everywhere, for example, the universal automobile and good highways have drained off much of the retail vitality of Hammondsport, leaving a very few basic stores and a succession of transient craft shops for the summer trade. Yet on balance the village at the end of the lake seems to me as blessed as it did when I was a boy.

You *can* go home again, of course, in the literal sense. And I am no longer so sure that you can't go home again in the sense Thomas Wolfe meant. But that is not really the question or the problem. What you can't do is discover the unchanged past. The past exists only as our particular memory of what was, and although there are fragments of it to be found, like shards of pottery in the sands of Mesopotamia, you are in the presence not of the past but of the inevitability, the inexorability, of change.

8

Still I go back when I can in quest of these shards of my past, and to see how much of the quality of village life has survived the sorry blandishments and the cruel exactments of progress.

Most often I fly to Rochester and rent a car and then drive south across the hills to Hammondsport. Each time I forget and have the pleasure of discovering all over again how beautiful western New York State is. Usually, with the time change from Los Angeles, it is dusk as I head out of the airport for open country, and the drive is like progressing from one page of a pictorial calendar to the next, each vista in the slanting light of late day more majestic than the last.

The new highway that leads from Bath north (but downhill most of the way) to Hammondsport is early postwar, which is no longer new, come to think of it. It commands an astonishing first glimpse of Lake Keuka, blue and cool at the foot of vineyarded hills.

The village clusters around the south end of Keuka, one of the handful of narrow, deep bodies of wonderfully clear water called the Finger Lakes that were clawed into the stony face of western New York by glaciers somewhat before my time.

Keuka is shaped like a Y and stretches twenty-two miles from Hammondsport on the south to Penn Yan (a contraction of "Pennsylvania Yankee") on the north, with a lovely wooded promontory called Bluff Point where the lake divides. As late as 1920 there were steamboats circling the lake, carrying passengers and freight (grapes in season) and summer excursionists.

The pioneer film producer Hal Roach, who put Laurel and Hardy together as a team and later invented the Our Gang comedies, was born in Elmira, New York, in 1892 and spent his early years there. He remembers how, when he was a child, his family would take the train to Bath, change to the B&H for the eight-mile ride down to Hammondsport and then enjoy an all-day outing on one of the lake steamers before heading back to Elmira. Alas, the last of the steamers burned at its dock a few years before I was born.

(In June, 1988, a prosperous local machinist and boat livery operator named Stanley Clark built and launched a diesel-powered, three-deck, 300-passenger excursion boat he named the *Keuka Maid*. It looks like a floating condominium but even so it catches something of the romantic old days.)

When I go back to Hammondsport, I swing off the new highway and take the old road, which is now heavily pot-holed, little-used, and narrower than ever, or so it feels. It leads past the New York State Fish Hatchery and the Pleasant Valley Cemetery and the two big wineries, Taylor and Pleasant Valley (old competitors, now two peas in the same corporate pod, first Coca-Cola, then Seagrams and now a new group called Vintners International).

I used to bicycle to Bath and back every Saturday to take a cornet lesson and catch a matinee at Schine's Babcock Theater, coasting all the way back down to Hammondsport and going like a bat out of hell. I saw every inch of the way as only a walker or a bike rider can.

Harry Benner's little snack shop near the fish hatchery is gone now, leveled, and no trace of it remains. He was already an old man, and very lame, in the days when I occasionally interrupted the climb to Bath to buy a candy bar from him. But I liked to stop because he was a historical figure. In his younger days he was a photographer and recorded many of the early flights of the fragile wood and canvas planes Glenn Curtiss was designing and building at Hammondsport, including the world's first seaplanes. I have many of Harry's photographs, printed up as post cards. G. H., as he was always called locally, and the other daring pioneer pilots stare solemnly or grin confidently for the camera. There are hundreds of other photographs by Harry Benner in the Curtiss Museum of Local History in the old all-grades stone schoolhouse where I started kindergarten. They are a priceless historical record, the life's work of a man who at the last sold candy bars.

Just beyond Harry's place was a farm which had a pigpen near the road and, as sure as spring, there would be a crop of

Stretching south from Hammondsport, Pleasant Valley lives up to its name. The buildings of the Taylor and Great Western wineries are clustered at the foot of the far hills. The field in the center was a landing ground for Glenn Hammond Curtiss's early airplanes.

piglets squealing around an enormous sow. I liked to take a breather and watch the action. Once, when I went back in the early seventies, the shed was still there, but the present farmer was raising goats instead of pigs, and there was a pair of kids in the pasture, frisking like children. When I went past again a few years later, the goats were gone too and the grass had taken over. The farm, like so many, had become a dwelling only.

The wineries used to sit at the west edge of the valley, their cellars carved out of the shale hills. In later years the companies have expanded across the valley floor, adding low, wide, industrial buildings through which the wine moves under automated controls.

Guided tours have grown to be a major summer selling device for the wineries, and there are tour buses and parking lots and a greensward where on summer Friday nights there are free concerts (with a complimentary glass of wine). The concerts under the stars, with crowds of hundreds sitting on blankets or lawn chairs they've fetched along, are one of the strong plusses of what I think of as The Later Hammondsport.

The special aroma of wine in the making is cool, damp, spiky, and strangely nostalgic and melancholy, as if it were wafting not out of the buildings but out of the past. The fragrance is a little harder to detect than it used to be, yet it still hangs lightly on the summer air when the conditions are right and, catching the scent of it as you drive by slowly with the window open, you know you have come home.

Once upon a childhood, well into the thirties, the grapes were hand-picked into wooden trays and hauled down from the steep vineyards above the lake on horse-drawn wagons that clanked through town on iron rims. The wagons moved so slowly that even a boy of only moderate speed could dash out and seize a bunch or two of Concords or Delawares or Iveses, while the driver cursed in only half-serious anger and brandished a whip much too short to reach the length of the wagon.

These days the grapes are for the most part no longer hand-picked but shaken off the vines by huge machines that suggest perverse and giant praying mantises from a horror movie. The grapes arrive at the presses in large unromantic bins aboard trucks. Like the rest of the wine-making, it is all very industrial.

Yet during harvest time, from late September through October and even into early November, there is that other unique winery smell, of fresh-squeezed grape juice. When the wind is out of the south, the aroma drifts down the valley to town like a wispy and magic perfume.

Perfume is probably the right word. It struck me once that the aroma of the wineries is a little like the faint trace of a sachet left in a box of old love letters. It conjures up images of a vanished day, in this case an earlier day when the wine-making gave Hammondsport in every sense a European flavor. Beyond the wineries the old Bath road becomes Lake Street, which indeed runs straight to the lake and is one of the two axes of the town, Main Street being the other.

I drive past the Lake Street house where I lived until I was sixteen. I've only been inside the house once since we left in 1942. The present owners, Willard and Rosalie Cummin, invited my sons and me to come in when we were on a family visit to Hammondsport in the seventies. The Cummins had added a bomb shelter in the nervous 1950s and a brick birdbath, where a climbable lilac tree used to stand, conceals its air vent. But the living room was so familiar that the whole house seemed full of ghosts and echoes and I found I was so moved I could scarcely speak. The past may fade but it never relaxes its hold.

I turn left onto Main Street, at the intersection they still call the monument corner, although the Civil War monument that used to stand where Lake and Main meet has since been moved onto the lawn of the old stone schoolhouse where the Curtiss Museum, the public library and the village offices are now. Shifting the monument must have been a logistical nightmare; I wish I had been there to watch it. The statue was always a traffic hazard, even in the days of horses and buggies. It was hell for automobiles, and out-of-town drivers used to come upon it with a great screeching of brakes. If there was no crash, the lads at the gas station on one corner would say, "Damn. Wasn't timed quite right."

From Main I turn down Sheather Street to the village square. I always feel two very special tugs here. In the center of the park is the ornate old green bandstand where I used to play in the town band on Saturday nights in the summertime. It is not used now, but it has been kept nicely painted and in good repair, in

The Civil War monument used to stand where Lake and
Main meet. It has since been moved onto the lawn of the
old stone schoolhouse. *Courtesy Glenn H. Curtiss Museum
of Local History*

case the past returns. The benches along the sides were removed
when the stand was restored as a civic beautification project, but
one quiet summer afternoon on an earlier visit I went up on the
stand and sat where I had sat, on the leader's right, and let the
echoes of marches, overtures, and medleys sound faintly but un-
forgettably in the mind's ear. Getting into the band was my first

triumph in what I thought of as the real world and I was proud of it for a long time. What am I saying? I still am.

Across the street from the bandstand, on the north side of the green, the Park Theater used to stand. Another lump in the throat. It was there I saw my first movie, an event as sharp in memory as today's breakfast, possibly sharper.

Steep roads lead north from town through the vineyarded hills on both sides of the lake. One morning on a visit to Hammondsport a few years ago I drove up the steeply winding Middle Road on the west side of the lake, which as I climbed glimmered far below me. I was on a personal pilgrimage and, trusting to very old recollection, looked for the dirt road (if it was still dirt, and it was) that turned off the blacktop, dipped down and across a gully, and became little more than a track through the vineyards.

I had remembered correctly and found my way to the J. D. Masson place, a stone farmhouse that had been built by my great-grandfather's cousin in I suppose the late 1860s. The house and the vineyards had been recently bought by Taylor Wine, and the house was empty because, I guessed, it was too expensive to heat in the winter. I parked the rented car and peeked in the windows.

Each fall when I was a boy, J. D.'s daughter, Aunt Lucie Carpenter, came east from Moorpark, California, where she raised walnuts, to supervise the grape-picking with the family who tended the vineyards for her. While she was here, Aunt Lucie gave an annual harvest luncheon on the lawn for the whole family. It was a meal that ranked with Thanksgiving and Christmas in the numbing abundance of food, ice cream, cake, and of course grapes just picked from the vines.

That morning the empty house looked strangely like a lost piece of Europe, half hidden by maple trees. The stillness was broken by far-off gunshots and a curious keening sound, like a Moog Synthesizer being tested. I learned later that the make-believe shots and the noise were devices, invented in California, to frighten the birds away from the grapes. I stood in the gently-

15

decaying barn where my brother and I used to play during the picnic. I listened to the ghostly wailing, compliments of California, and drove back to town.

I have occasionally said, as a joke, that Hammondsport was a resort town—people would resort to anything to get away from it. But it was only a joke. I always thought it was a terrific place to live, and in my early days I was more intimidated than tempted by the thought of leaving. What displaces us all from our origins, love them or not, is that so often you have to move on to find the kind of work you want to do for a living, which in my case was to write. But in the fullness of time we may just reverse the process and resort to anything to get home again.

I never came home to Hammondsport without a tumbling rush of emotions: gratitude that so much of it is as I remember it and a stinging awareness that all the changes and all the absences measure how many of my own years have become memory.

The Village

Even now, dropping down into Hammondsport from high on one of the surrounding hills, it's easy to see what the first settlers saw in the late eighteenth century: a broad, green, fertile, stream-divided valley ideal for farming and livestock, hills thick with trees for lumber and a long lake that was undoubtedly full of fish, but that more importantly was to be a perfect artery of transportation in a land that would be short of roads for some time to come.

The word about the narrow, clear blue lakes and the rich valleys had been spread by the soldiers of General John Sullivan, who marched through the countryside fighting Indians loyal to the British during the Revolution.

The first settlers, William Aulls and his son Tom, arrived on foot in 1793, and another small group at the end of winter in 1794. That group included my great-great-great-grandfather Sam Baker, his wife, and four of their eventually twelve children, his wife's parents, and one of Sam's Revolutionary War comrades who was on the lam from the state of Massachusetts for his part in Shays's Rebellion against taxes.

They established their homesteads along the stream, a little way up the valley from the lakefront. In 1796 a flamboyant character named Captain John Shether came along, acquired several acres of lakefront land, and built a store and a mill. But he overextended himself and had to sell everything to another man, who in turn sold the land to an 1807 arrival, Lazarus Hammond. Judge Hammond, as he was known, laid out the streets and the village square and gave the place his name.

George McClure, a general in the Revolutionary War, settled at Cold Springs, south of Pleasant Valley toward Bath, in 1802, built a saw mill and a flour mill and became an important wheat dealer. He erected the first warehouse in Hammondsport and, more significantly, commissioned a thirty-ton schooner called *Sally,* to haul wheat from Penn Yan to his warehouse. This became the first commercial craft on Crooked Lake (which was not renamed Keuka until the 1860s).

At first the grain was stored for the winter at Hammondsport. Then in the spring it was hauled by wagon upon a pine-plank road to Bath, where it was loaded on ark-boats on the Cohocton River to begin the long water journey that ended at Philadelphia or Baltimore. Later, in 1830, the Crooked Lake Canal from Penn Yan to Seneca Lake linked Hammondsport with the Erie Canal, and the town continued to enjoy a considerable (although, as it turned out, temporary) boom as a busy port.

The late Laura Swarthout, whose brief history of Hammondsport is still the standard document, wrote, "Long lines of produce-bearing wagons waited their turns at the docks. Warehouses and dry docks lined the lake edge. Stores, small factories, mills and cafes clustered around Water Street. Water Street was the commercial heart of the village until one disastrous fire after another caused many of the proprietors to seek the safer neighborhood around Pulteney Park [the village square]" (p. 5). An 1879 history of Steuben County added that "many speculators and capitalists were attracted to the place, and many investments made which subsequently proved worthless" (Clayton, p. 413). But as part of the transportation boom, the first steamboat, the *Keuka,* the Indian name for the lake, was launched in 1835, followed in later years by the *Yates* and the *Steuben.* The largest of the lake steamers, the *Mary Bell,* which was later rechristened the *Penn Yan,* was one hundred fifty feet long and carried four hundred passengers.

I had no trouble imagining what the days of the steamers must have been like, with the whistles hooting and the band music echoing across the lake on a Sunday afternoon, and I was always convinced I'd been born a few decades too late.

The opening of the Erie Railroad in 1850 and the Corning-Rochester branch a few years later quickly deflated the boom. The flour and wool and timber could go east, mostly, or west by rail. Hammondsport's population had grown to around six hundred, but it leveled out for several years. For a time in the middle of the nineteenth century, according to one senior resident, Hammondsport was also known informally as Peg Town, because one of its small factories made wooden pegs for the construction of shoes and boots.

There were changes in the wind. The town's first Episcopal priest had shown that grapes flourished in the local limestone soil and in the local climate, on which the lake acted as a thermostat against too-early thaws in the spring and too-early frosts in the fall. By the 1850s grape-growing was a thriving local industry and table grapes (sometimes cooled by ice harvested from the lake in winter and stored in ice houses) were shipped to New York and other cities by the hundreds of pounds. Soon there were more grapes than the markets could absorb and in 1860 the first of the wineries was organized to make alternate use of them. Hammondsport, it turned out, had found its occupation.

The Bath & Hammondsport Railroad opened for business in 1874, carrying grapes and wine—and passengers. The passengers were mostly day-trippers who took the Erie or the Delaware, Lackawanna & Western trains from as far away as Elmira and Rochester, changing at Bath to the B&H for an outing on the steamers.

Glenn Hammond Curtiss, the local boy who built motorcycles and then airplanes, carved another niche in history for Ham-

A post card view of Hammondsport around the turn of the century showed one of the paddlewheel steamers at its pier. Virtually all the lakefront buildings are, like the steamers, long gone. *Courtesy Glenn H. Curtiss Museum of Local History*

mondsport. Part of his legacy, in my boyhood, was the unusual number of planes, including autogiros and snarling little racers, that seemed to fill the skies on summer days. The rest of the legacy was Mercury Aircraft, organized by three local men in 1920 to manufacture spare parts for the Curtiss Jenny (the JN4) which was the barnstormers' favorite in the first years after the war. Mercury also designed several airplanes of its own, but they were not successful commercially. The firm became a metal fabricator, making among other things computer housings for IBM and similar items for Kodak and other behemoths. Mercury is now by far Hammondsport's largest employer. Mercury is also privately owned, principally by the descendants of Joseph Meade, who was one of the founders and whose grandson is now one of its chief executives.

I had no reason to think of it at the time, but I realize now that local ownership, together with the hills, the lake, the grapes, the wine, and the airplanes, gave Hammondsport its unique character. You took it for granted that the Taylors, old Walter's descendants, owned the Taylor Wine Company, and that they all lived in town and rubbed elbows with their employees in the public library and the stores and at the gas stations. Slightly more exclusive elbows were rubbed at the Keuka Yacht Club and the all-male Glenwood Club on the east side of the lake, where the men took weekly turns cooking and serving the food and mixing the drinks. (Both clubs still flourish.)

In the same way the descendants of the original C. D. Champlin owned the controlling shares of the Pleasant Valley Wine Company, with an additional few shares in the family of Jules Masson, the longtime wine-maker (and another of my great-grandfathers). The Urbana Wine Company was Stuart Underhill, who had a lovely year-round lakeside home just across the highway from the winery, whose label was Gold Seal. Even though the Underhills also had a home in Corning and owned the newspaper there, the *Leader*, they still constituted local rather than absentee ownership. Mercury Aircraft *was* the elder Joe Meade, who was to be seen puttering in his yard on Main Street. The Putnam Wine Company (Golden Age) was Deyo W. "Put" Putnam, and so it went. The B&H was locally owned and the telephone company was, too.

It would not have occurred to me that nearly all those institutions would one day no longer be locally owned. Yet only the B&H and Mercury are still in local hands and only Mercury prospers. The wineries and the telephone company are absentee owned and in fact there is no longer a living telephone operator in Hammondsport—there is only a locked building in which clicking noises are heard. The first time I went back and discovered the absence of operators I felt more than a passage of time; it was as if a gulf had opened between the present and my past.

The effect of local ownership, I think now, had been to give Hammondsport an identity and a solidarity, a sense (that was felt if not voiced) that the town was in no way a satellite, an outpost dependent on the mercies of some elsewhere-dwelling THEM. We were, so it felt, a self-contained, self-sufficient world within the world.

It was slightly a myth, naturally; we were at the mercy of the marketplace, of foreign nations and our own government (as Prohibition painfully proved). The larger world intruded whether we wanted it to (in the form of movies, for example) or whether we didn't (in the form of war and taxes). Yet the decisions about the wineries were made by neighbors until the 1960s, and for years Arthur Moore *was* the Hammondsport Telephone Company and you could take complaints right to him (or tell Central to tell him). Now Hammondsport goes elsewhere to do much of its shopping, and the fate of its major wineries is determined in New York City.

If we were once a self-contained world, or seemed to be, we were also a stable and homogeneous world. The village is no longer quite so settled (what village is?) but it is, so I judge, still remarkably homogeneous.

The melting pot may have done its melting, but there were relatively few ingredients to begin with—English, Irish, Scotch, French, German, Swiss, Italian, Polish, but predominately Anglo-Saxon. It would be too kind to say that there were no ethnic or other prejudices lurking in Hammondsport. You heard the racial tags and the wisps of conversation which as much as anything simply *assumed* a differentness from the ethnic masses of the cities. (The cities, New York in particular, were thought of with a mixture of awe, fear, and suspicion by those who had seldom if ever been there, which was almost everybody.)

22

But the lurking prejudices were seldom exercised because there was seldom any occasion. There were only two black families in town. George Jones and his wife and daughter ran a barber shop and beauty parlor upstairs over the Park Theater. They lived in a house across the street from the Catholic Church. They were as quietly middle class as it was possible to be; their clientele was white because there was no other. You thought of them not as Negroes but as neighbors.

The other black woman in Hammondsport was called Black Eva, but I learned later that this was simply to distinguish her from my father's imperious Aunt Eva Champlin, for whom Black Eva did the cooking for dinner parties. (My great-aunt was not called White Eva, although later she acquired the nickname Birdie.) The name Black Eva now seems patronizing in a way it didn't in the thirties. She was a free spirit, slight and gray-haired and apparently ageless, who lived in a tiny house down at the lakefront and cooked for several families in town. I am discomfited now, thinking about Eva and her shacky life in the low land between Howell's Lumber Yard and the lake. But Eva was loved, in a tradition that was I suppose more Southern than Northern.

There was, so far as I recall, only one Jewish family in town. Harry Cohen, a businessman from New York, ran a small winery operation. His granddaughter, Gladys, was in my class in high school and had a lively and impish sense of humor that would have defeated any hostility, if there'd been any.

For a short time the Board of Education hired a principal who was Jewish. He did not stay long, but it would require impartial adult testimony from the period to say exactly why he left. His manner was abrupt, abrasive, and authoritative, which I would now recognize as a kind of offensive defense common to big city life and appropriate to hostile surroundings elsewhere, though not ideal in a placid upstate town in the thirties. Whether anti-Semitism was at the root of his leaving or whether it was the non-denominational culture shock of the city-bred man amid alien corn or whether he just wasn't a very good principal (a position in which a gift for public relations is requisite), I don't know. My retrospective hunch is that there were elements of all three, and a further hunch is that he left in anger and disappointment and without regret.

Then as now Hammondsport was a pretty place, not so manicured as to be picture-book pretty, but a village of tree-shaded streets and predominantly clapboard houses of two and three stories, with others of brick and masonry and at least one, old and classic, of cobblestone. Many of the fine old elms are gone but the maples are ancient and tall.

The lakefront has been beautified and the business section looks spiffier than it has in years. There is a tidy motel where Putnam's dock and some decaying storage sheds—mementos of the lake-traffic days—used to stand. The developers have their eye on the village, and there is a lively fight over a proposal to build blocks of condominiums down at the lakefront. The price of shoreline property has gone sky-high. The traffic thunders along Route 54 on the east side of the lake night and day.

There are major and minor changes to be noted. The new high school stands where the old village ball diamond was and where cows grazing were a hazard for center fielders. Hammondsport had a woman mayor for years, and the new pastor of St. James's Episcopal Church is a woman. The wineries turn out wine coolers as well as champagne, to the disgust of the purists. There is a cable system and a video rental store.

Yet a former resident can sit on the cottage porch of an early evening and look at the green geometry of the vineyards on the hillside across the lake and see the lights of the village in the distance, breathe the smog-free air and hear the cicadas' song and imagine that nothing has changed at all.

Sam Baker

The farther away from me it is in both years and miles, the more clearly I see Hammondsport as a case history of the American founding experience. My great-great-great-grandfather Sam Baker and the other early settlers of the town were walking embodiments of the westering spirit that kept pushing into the wilderness which lay beyond the existing settlements.

The original Jeffrey, or Geoffrey, Champlin, who landed in Rhode Island about 1650 and from whom, through his three sons, all the American Champlins are descended, is his own version of the American experience. The genealogists can trace his tribe westward to the Pacific Coast like a widening migration. But Sam Baker, whose granddaughter married one of those westering Champlins, has always been my window on the early days.

His early life reads like the synopsis of a Walter D. Edmonds novel. It was first set to paper in 1914 by one of Sam's innumerable descendants, Judge Frank Baker of Chicago.

In 1777 Sam, who was then fourteen, and his brother William and their father Jonathan were living in White Creek (now Salem), New York, near Albany. On an August afternoon of that Revolutionary War year the boys were out picking berries. William spotted a couple of Indians and whispered a warning to Sam. Sam stood up for a better look and was captured. The two Indians, whose loyalties were with the British, argued over what

25

to do with the boy. The younger Indian favored scalping him on the spot. The older Indian reasoned that the lad might be salable, and his wisdom prevailed. They took Sam and headed off toward the British lines. General John Burgoyne had captured Fort Edwards near Glens Falls on July 26 and was advancing on Albany.

That night the Indians killed a deer and made a stew, flavoring it, so Sam said later, with baby robins. He remembered it as the best meal he ever had—certainly the most gratefully received. They reached Burgoyne's camp the next day, and the Indians sold Sam to one of Burgoyne's officers for the equivalent of twelve dollars. Sam was put to work in the officers' mess, and there he stayed until Burgoyne surrendered to General Horatio Gates at Saratoga a few weeks later, in October, 1777. After the surrender, which Sam witnessed, an American officer gave Sam two dollars and told him to get home while the getting was good. Sam went back to White Creek but in 1781, when he turned eighteen, he enlisted in Captain Peter Van Rensselaer's company, which was part of a force under Colonel Marinus Willett assigned to protect the northwest frontier of New York State. Sam saw action at Johnstown and West Canada Creek in October of that year.

After the war Sam married Elizabeth Daniels of Hudson, New York, the daughter of an unreconstructed Tory who had spent the war on British turf in New York City. Now the war was over, and in 1787 Sam headed west to make his fortune. Travelling by foot and river raft, he and a fellow Revolutionary War veteran, Amos Stone, took the North Branch of the Susquehanna River to the mouth of the Chemung at Tioga Point, poled along the Chemung to Painted Post, swung on to the Tioga and followed it to its junction with the Cowanesque, just south of the New York state line. There they build a cabin, tethered the cow they had brought with them, and planted corn. They were the first settlers in the Tioga Valley.

They acquired an Indian handyman, and before the snow came Sam left Stone in charge and retraced his steps to Hudson, where he spent the winter. In the spring he returned to Tioga with Elizabeth and their infant daughter, Mary, and his in-laws, Mr. and Mrs. Richard Daniels. Elizabeth was pregnant with their second child. There were some tense moments, Sam remembered, when they neared the clearing because at first there wasn't a living soul in sight. But Amos, the Indian, and the cow all turned out to be fine.

The Bakers, the Danielses and Amos Stone spent six years in the Tioga Valley and the next three of the Bakers' twelve children—Caty, Tryphena and William—were born there. It is to be noted, as the family genealogy does, that all twelve of the Baker children—six sons and six daughters—grew to adulthood and produced a total of eighty-four grandchildren for Sam and Elizabeth. Elizabeth Daniels Baker would obviously be worth a biography or a novel in her own right.

They might have stayed on, but trouble developed over the title to their land. (It was in western Pennsylvania, but the land at that moment seemingly belonged to Connecticut.) Lacking a clear title, Sam got ready to pioneer again. According to Frank Baker's history, Sam had walked all the way from Pennsylvania to Canandaigua, New York, to have a rifle repaired, and had passed through the then-uninhabited Pleasant Valley and liked it.

A Revolutionary War figure, Colonel Charles Williamson, was headquartered at Bath, New York, and acting as land agent for the thousands of acres in western New York that had been the estate of Sir William Pulteney before the war. From Williamson Sam Baker obtained a grant of three hundred acres in Pleasant Valley by a deed dated December 9, 1793. The land flanked what is now called Cold Springs Inlet and stretched across the valley floor to the hills. Sam brought Elizabeth and the family up from Tioga the following spring. Amos Stone and the Danielses acquired parcels nearby and settled in.

(The angers of war last long after hostilities end. Sam's father-in-law Daniels never signed an oath of allegiance to the new nation and vowed to resettle in Canada. His wife warned him she would leave him if he did, so he stayed on in Pleasant Valley, an embittered old man never popular with his grandchildren, according to Frank Baker's history.)

Sam built the first frame house in the valley, erected a mill beside the Cold Springs Inlet and created a large and prosperous farm. He also became politically active. He was first a Jeffersonian Republican and then a Whig, a friend of John Jay, an opponent of DeWitt Clinton and the Erie Canal. The new town of Bath south of the valley made him its first assessor. Later he was named Steuben County's first judge of the court of common pleas and finally its first surrogate judge.

Sam was a great letter-writer, and in his senior years he gave his children prudent advice on how to conduct their lives. "Now Richard," he wrote to one of his sons, "as you lay the foundation so will the building be strong or weak. One thing I would impress on your mind—it is much easier to be what you would wish people to think you are than to make them believe you are what you are not. It is very easy to practice Justice, Mercy and Love and Truth but very hard to make people believe you are an honest man without being in reality such."

Sam Baker lived into his eighty-second year, a patriarchal figure who looked the part. He had a massive head and weighed more than two hundred pounds although he was well short of six feet tall. He died in 1842 and is buried in Pleasant Valley Cemetery, within a few hundred yards of his homestead.

Another of the early settlers was Lazarus Hammond, who came to the valley from Dansville, New York, in 1808, bought a tract of land at the lake front, divided it into lots, donated a piece of land for the village square, and named the town Hammondsport.

Hammond's daughter Catherine married one of Sam Baker's sons, also named Samuel, and one of young Samuel and Catherine's daughters, named Emily, in 1847 married a rising young Hammondsport merchant named Charles Davenport Champlin,

28

who had come to town from Stamford, New York, in 1844 to work for his cousin A. M. Adsit, in a canal warehouse.

Some of this, quite a lot of it, I knew when I was growing up in Hammondsport. Much of the genealogy could be read across the gravestones in Pleasant Valley Cemetery. The presence of the past, which can be seen and felt in the ancient cities of Europe, could be felt in Hammondsport as well, even nearer and more intimate. Children live in the moment, not much troubled or impressed by past or future, but I came to feel later in life that this sense of the past I acquired early was one of the things that made growing up in Hammondsport special. And the more I knew about the family past, the more clearly I understood why I felt so much a part of Hammondsport, and Hammondsport so much a part of me.

I sometimes try to imagine Sam Baker, full of years and wisdom, sitting in the shade on a warm summer afternoon, letting the days of his Indian captivity drift through memory, or seeing again the silent wilderness as he poled up the Tioga. And I think of him trying to imagine what the lives of his grandchildren's children would be like, and figuring that that was their worry; he had done his best.

Overtown

A child of the city would prob-
ably have found it preposterous that anybody could get excited
about walking overtown in the Hammondsport of the 1930s.
"Overtown," as in "You wanna go overtown?," was the business
section of Hammondsport in the 1930s. It covered hardly more
than five blocks altogether, circling three sides of the village
square and part of the fourth, with some short extensions into
the side streets.

But being allowed to walk overtown, unescorted, was one of
the earliest pleasures and the earliest adventure I can remember.
It was, in the beginning, always an errand: to pick up a prescription at the drug store, get the mail, a loaf of bread, a quart
of ice cream. No matter; it was a chance to go where Hammondsport bustled, insofar as it ever bustled.

A tourist driving through the Finger Lakes region might have
found the business section folksy, but not quaint in the neat antiquarian way the New England villages further east are quaint.
There was no bypass around Hammondsport, no way to avoid
making a slow drive around the square and through the town.
The impatient tourist might not even have been willing to call us
folksy, despite the gingerbread bandstand in the park.

The overtown architecture was late Victorian, turn-of-the-
century commercial Americana, a mixture of three-story business blocks of red brick and of clapboard stores two stories high,

The turn-of-the-century bandstand in the village square, Pulteney Park, where I played many Saturday night concerts with the town band, has been wonderfully restored but, alas, there are no longer any regular concerts. The Bank of Hammondsport is at the rear.

with apartments upstairs. The Presbyterian Church with its tall steeple and the Hammondsport Hotel with its long lobby window faced each other on opposite sides of the park. Both were built of white clapboard that gleams in memory as it did in life, and they dominated the square.

It was only three blocks from our house on Lake Street to the stores, and I knew every crack in the sidewalks. Cement was beginning to replace the original stone slabs. I often make that journey in memory, triggered by some piece of news from Hammondsport. These days, in consequence of my California years, I am not so much the walker as a witnessing camera, following the short, thin boy in corduroy knickers, although the observer and the boy share the same recollections and the feelings.

I pass the Atlantic gas station, which was to become a hang-out in my earlier teenage years, and I cross Main Street to run my hand along the cool pipe of the schoolhouse fence.

(A specific memory intrudes: I am learning to rollerskate and clinging to the railing for support. Then I recall the late fall day when I had finally got the hang of skating. I could take long, gliding, confident, strides instead of short, slow feints that weren't much better than walking. I skated over to the school to show off, ignoring the fact that it had started to snow. When I got there the wheels would hardly turn for the wet snow that was clogging them. Nobody else was skating; they'd put their skates away for the winter. I felt like a proper idiot, a common experience.)

On my tracking shot through memory I turn at the school and cross Lake Street, pausing to look in on the Deluxe Ice Cream stand which one of the Carlson boys operated for a while. Their chocolate chip was worth every cent of a week's allowance. The stand was attached to Love's Restaurant, which was torn down while I still lived in Hammondsport and replaced by a gas station, which survives.

Occasionally, disobeying orders, I used to cross the intersection diagonally so I could climb on the Civil War statue of Monroe Brundage, who stands forever with his musket at the ready, bayonet fixed. The older, wiser me says it was a damned fool thing to do. The cars tore around the monument, blindly indifferent to what was happening on the far side. But in those days it was merely an adventure. Later on, we would sit on the monument watching the cars come at us.

Memory pauses again beneath the trees in front of the narrow brown house on Main Street where Doc LaCelle, the town dentist, had his first office. Just there, one night when I was in sixth grade, I was walking a girl home from the movies when one of our classmates jumped out from behind a tree and shouted that she was *his* girl. He grabbed me by the lapels of my winter jacket and I was so startled and scared that I roared with outrage and pushed him away with a punch to the chest, which must have startled him because the last thing in the world I had was a reputation as a fighter.

We yelled at each other for a while and he went away when the girl explained that we were all just friends, which was approximately true. But the surge of adrenaline had me quivering for an hour. It was my first object lesson in the way romance can complicate your life even when it's *not* serious.

Sheather Street (a misspelling of Old John Shether's name) is the main drag of the business section. It slopes gently down toward the lakefront. All the streets in town slope either north to the lakefront or east to the Inlet. There's hardly a street in Hammondsport that is level for more than a couple of blocks.

At the top of Sheather Street is the Frey Block, which was built in 1901 by a local family of winemakers who had come originally from Germany. They designed it with stores on the ground floor and a small but elegant opera house which occupied most of the second and third floors.

By the time I was growing up, the opera house had been closed for a long time, condemned because it had inadequate fire exits. It was evidently only used for two decades or so. I've regretted all my life that I was never able to get inside and look around, because the idea of an opera house is magical. I'm sure I could have detected the ghostly emanations of an ancient coloratura or an itinerant lecturer on the Holy Land, with slides.

I have seen a photograph of a splendid carriage delivering passengers for the night's entertainment and parked before the iron stairs that led to the opera house, which was entered on the

On a summer afternoon in 1949, Hammondsport's principal business street, Sheather, was not quite bustling. Jim Smellie's Drug Store, next to the Police and Fire Departments and below the Masonic rooms, was one of the nerve centers of the village. The picture is one I took, trying out a new camera during a brief vacation.

second floor. In other photographs the proscenium stage looks to have been a jewel, likelier to accommodate recitals than grand opera, but a proud gesture of local cultural aspirations.

The only remaining external signs of the opera house are tall doors, now bricked in, on the rear wall where scenery was admitted. A young couple purchased the whole Frey building a few years ago, opened the opera house for a last party, and then

34

The Frey Building, in right foreground at the top of Sheather Street, contained a small and charming opera house when it was built in 1901. But a few years later the auditorium was shut down by fire laws and no trace of it remains.

stripped the interior, which was converted to apartments. Near the top of the building's front facade, windblown seeds have taken root in crevices and become straggly weeds. There were retail stores on the ground floor: a hardware store that provided my first small bicycle and my first and only pair of skis, a small five-and-dime and, for several years, the public library.

On down Sheather was Ethel Wooding's dry goods shop with its skeins of yarn and its gentle aroma of sachet. I always felt uncomfortable in Mrs. Wooding's, which was obviously a place for women, as hardware stores were places for men. But there were items of interest, like the yardstick attached to the counter and the adroit speed with which Mrs. Wooding or her clerk could unwind and measure yards of material from the bolts of cloth.

Some of the storefronts had a kind of fugitive life, changing identities with the rise and fall of economic fortune. Beyond the dry goods store was the A&P which is now a hardware store. There was a narrow vacant lot behind a board fence. Then came Pete Kapral's jewelry store, where at an early age I helped sell fireworks. Next to Pete's was Clarence Payne's meat market. The post office was next, beside a stone-paved alley that led to the livery stables behind the stores. When the post office moved to larger quarters down the street, the space became another grocery store.

After the alley there was the one-truck firehouse where the noon siren blew and then Smellie's Rexall Drug Store. The post office was one of the nerve centers in town, but Smellie's ran it a close second. Even as I write the name I realize how oddly it will read. Smellie is a good old Scots name and Jim's father, who came from Canada, had had the drug store before him, so we never thought twice about it. The truth is that one of the treats of youth was a cherry Coke at the marble fountain at Smellie's. Jim was also Western Union and had transmitted hundreds of dispatches for reporters who had come to watch Glenn Curtiss's flights. He was the newspaper outlet in town, and when I delivered papers I picked up my bundles at Smellie's.

Next to Smellie's was the town's oldest hardware store, Freidell and Lacher's. Like all good hardware stores, it was a wonderment of tools, paints, rope, nails in open kegs, and Things for every need and function the mind of man could devise. I could hardly pound a nail or make a straight saw-cut, but I always wanted one of everything in the store.

Marsh Rouin's Park Inn—dining room, a few guest rooms and a bar—contended with the tavern at the Hammondsport Hotel as the most popular saloon in town once Prohibition was over. Marsh, born Marcel, was a tall, slim, bald Frenchman who grew grapes across the valley from town. His two sons are contemporaries of mine and one of them, Wally, was a precocious raconteur with a fine gift of exaggeration. His tales of the mad-cap antics in the bar were mostly myth, I'm sure, but they increased the fascination and the mystery of a place that was, naturally, off limits to me. I was in my forties when, on a summer vacation, I first went into the bar at the Park Inn and, after all those years, I still felt as if I were seeing a lodge's forbidden chamber.

Markle's Meat Market, now an ice cream parlor, really *was* a meat market, with chopping blocks and sawdust on the floor and no shrink-wrapped mini-steaks or any other pre-packaged meats to be found. The sides of beef came in the back door, went into the cold storage chamber, and were subsequently operated upon by Mr. Markle and his slow-moving assistant Dusty Rhodes in full view of the customers. I don't know that I'm a better person for having watched the two of them do their meat-cutting chores, but it beats thinking that Mother Nature puts the chops in those cute packages.

The Union Block was the second of Hammondsport's office buildings, with the volunteer fire department's Hook and Ladder rooms on the top floor, lawyers and insurance agents on the second and, on the street level, M. Cohn & Sons' clothing store, Horace Sirrine's insurance office, the Gent's Club barber shop and pool parlor (hunting and fishing licenses sold) and, on the corner, the Park Pharmacy, run by Maurice Hoyt in most of the years I knew it. The Park was the magazine outlet in town. It carried the slick weeklies and monthlies, but it also had six wide shelves of the pulp magazines. I was a frequent visitor, quite early, because the pulps, like *The Shadow* and *Doc Savage*, were my introduction to grown-up reading.

The Hook and Ladder rooms were used for dances and for Robert Hallenbeck's dancing school. It was there I learned very quickly that tap dancing was not for me.

Across the corner from the pharmacy stood George H. Fay's grocery, which was darker and more interestingly aromatic than the other food stores in town. It was also independent, not a chain store managed by local people. It seems in memory to have been the most traditional of the grocery stores, with barrels and bags of bulk products and not just packaged foods. It closed and became the site of the new post office.

Diagonally opposite the drug store stood the imposing three-story Hammondsport Hotel, with its upper floors overhanging the street and forming a columned arcade of sorts. Visitors sat in a line of overstuffed leather chairs in the lobby to watch the passing parade. The floor was a mosaic of small hexagonal tiles, white with designs in black, which always struck me as very elegant. The Emilsons, a Swedish family, owned and operated the hotel. Rudolph was the patriarch, and his sons Norm and Herb both played in the town band. Herb ran the tavern and Norm was the station agent at the B&H Railroad.

To give the women in the family a break from the kitchen, my great-uncle Victor would occasionally treat all of us to Sunday dinner at the hotel. The fricassee chicken with biscuits was the best I ever ate. We were usually served by a cheerful and buxom blonde waitress who stirred all kinds of premature yearnings within me.

Along the street from the hotel, past a storefront that had had several identities, none very successful, stood the blessed Park Theater, where I was introduced to the movies. Grimaldi's Restaurant, with its marble soda fountain, its green booths and a year-round window display of Whitman's chocolates, was at the corner. Mrs. Grimaldi's moist chocolate cake ruined more diets than any other concoction in Steuben County, and her tuna salad sandwiches were a symphony of high cholesterol (as I would think now), swimming in mayonnaise and unutterably fine.

I took my first serious date to a movie (title long forgotten) and then to Grimaldi's for a milkshake. In my nervousness I dumped the container into her lap. Joan, who was slightly older and vastly more sophisticated, made light of it, but it delayed the onset of savoir-faire for years.

Across the corner from Grimaldi's was a two-story wooden block which, in the days I am recalling, contained the Keuka Restaurant, run by a Greek immigrant named Athan Carrasas, his wife Mary, and their five children. Next door to it was John Frisk's barber shop, which also offered pool tables at the back. The telephone office was upstairs over the barber shop, along with some small apartments. In one of them lived a retired free-lance winemaker named Leander Lane, who kept all his worldly possessions in a heavy iron-bound wooden captain's chest. Once, when I was in the town band, Leander dug down into the chest and pulled out a fine old fluegelhorn he used to play. I have wondered what became of it.

For years Leander kept company with Nettie Webster, who did most of the town's baking. I used to go with my cart to pick up dinner rolls and bread when my grandmother was having a dinner party. It was an assignment I loved because Nettie's kitchen smelled so delicious.

The joke was that after thirty years Leander had said, "Nettie, let's be wed," and Nettie had replied, "Don't be silly, Leander; who'd have us?" It is, I now think, a universal joke which I've heard about other couples in other places. They never did wed.

Just past Bob Staats' liquor store and Carl Eckert's grocery stood another business block, this one containing Fred and Charlie Faucett's furniture store and funeral parlor and Roma Marsh's beauty salon. One dramatic night the furniture store and the beauty parlor went up in a fire that could be seen for miles—fed, so we heard, by the supplies of embalming fluid. Why the whole business section didn't burn as well I don't know.

At the top of the square sat (and sits) the red brick Bank of Hammondsport (now a branch of Chase-Lincoln) and the Presbyterian Church. Mrs. Velie had a notions shop around the corner from the Park Pharmacy; it was from her that we bought our caps and cap pistols. Across the street from her Ray Smith had a shoe repair shop.

Overtown seemed to a child to offer almost everything you could want, except maybe a toy store. But once there had been even more businesses. Not long ago one of the town's unofficial historians, Maurice Hoyt Jr., the son of the pharmacist, jotted down a list of the businesses he remembered or had records of from 1900 to 1929.

As late as World War I, Hoyt wrote, there were four hotels in Hammondsport. (In the end fire claimed them all. The history of the development of small towns all over the country is written in fire.) There were, he said, two livery stables, five grocery stores *and* five meat markets, three blacksmith shops, five barber shops, not one but three movie houses, three millinery stores, three pool halls, two men's clothing stores, twelve wineries, a cooperage shop, five grape-packing houses, a grist mill, three lumber yards, four coal yards, three doctors, two dentists, a chiropractor and a veterinarian and a harness shop. Also, of course, an airplane works (Glenn Curtiss's company), a motorcycle factory, five insurance agents and three lawyers.

There was a unique industry, Dick Aber's Wire Hood factory. The wire hoods were the ones that secure the corks in champagne. It was said to be one of only three manufacturers of wire hoods in the world, with another in France and another in California. Women turned out the hoods by the thousands on a piece-work basis. The hoods are still used—removing them is part of the champagne rituals—but the factory in Hammondsport closed years ago.

The number of local businesses had clearly declined a lot by the mid-thirties and has shrunk even more since. I was growing up at the end of one era and the beginning of another. Hammondsport might have changed even faster except that Prohibition and the Depression slowed everything down. The Second

World War became a benchmark, dividing past from future, with a big assist from the automobile, easy credit, and prosperity.

Distances began to be measured in time, not miles, and the time kept shrinking. The shopping malls are only a quarter-hour away in Bath and only a little farther away in Corning and Elmira. Hammondsport as a place to shop is still self-contained in the sense that the necessities of daily living are all near at hand. If anybody still walks overtown instead of popping into the car, and I assume a few people still do, you can buy audio and rent video cassettes and at least a limited choice of new books. You still can't buy a fur coat and attend a chiropodist, nor, I think, acquire a man's suit or a pair of dress shoes. I counted only two grocery stores the last time I looked, but there are still two hardware stores. There hasn't been a movie house in years, although there is a radio station in Bath.

I try not to surrender to nostalgia. Yet it appears to me that there really is a difference between then and now, and that it is measured by more than the goods and services you can't buy locally, or by the disappearance of the livery stables. The spiritual difference is, so to speak, that overtown is a neighborhood, suburban shopping center in just the way it was not in the old days. It caters to tourists and summer cottagers, which gives it a distinctive flavor, but in its stores as in its employment Hammondsport is no longer quite so free-standing.

There is a subtle question, which I can't answer, and it is whether Hammondsport has the same strong sense of community that it did when it was so much more self-contained and self-sufficient. There is evidence both ways. The public library has great trouble finding volunteers and funds, although this (sadly enough) may say more about the larger society in the television/VCR age than about Hammondsport specifically. The fraternal orders continue to meet and elect regularly. To what extent they prosper and grow or to what extent they are a fading vestige of a different time the election notices do not reveal.

On the other hand, the volunteer firemen and the volunteer ambulance corps are large and effective organizations, more numerous and ambitious than ever. The firemen have funded and built an elaborate four- or five-truck station near the head of the lake. The ambulance operates from a splendid brick building where the Carrasas's Keuka Restaurant once stood. The high school band, which now takes statewide prizes for its precision drills, has fervent community support. There are no regular concerts in the park but there is an annual weekend arts and crafts show that draws a throng.

I have no doubt that I would be glad and comfortable to be back, electing to walk overtown on those root-heaved sidewalks, picking up the mail, and shopping as I could. But I would agitate like mad to stir up support for the library.

Growing Up

The house I grew up in still stands, quite unchanged on the outside, at 51 Lake Street. It sits at the corner of Orchard Street, which was dirt when I lived there but is now blacktopped. The house is a compact two-story plus attic structure of white clapboard. There are traces of the Greek Revival influence in the white columns on the front porch and in the roof line, the trademarks of a wandering carpenter who paused in Hammondsport in the 1870s and built several houses.

There are a living room, dining room, den, bathroom and kitchen downstairs and three bedrooms and another bathroom upstairs. Over the years the house had settled noticeably, and if you dropped a marble in the living room it would roll all the way back to the kitchen. Our rent was $22.50 a month and our landlords, Charles and Margaret Younglove, lived just behind us on Orchard Street. Their daughter, Rosalie, and her husband Willard Cummin have lived in the house since we left in 1942 and they had the floors re-leveled.

Mine was the middle bedroom upstairs, with windows on two sides and a window bench and bookcases on the south side. It was a wonderful room to read in, and if a welcoming atmosphere can create a love of reading, I owe everything to that bedroom.

There was also a cellar, dirt-floored and with a ceiling so low that even an average-sized man had to stoop. The furnace was

My house at 51 Lake Street is essentially unchanged, although the lilac tree I climbed on in the side yard is gone, replaced by a brick birdbath which conceals the vent for an air raid shelter added in the nervous fifties.

in a kind of hollow that had been dug out a foot deeper than the rest of the cellar. Most of my memories of the cellar revolve around that furnace. No one who has not tended a coal-burning furnace—shaken its grates, started it from scratch when it went out, shovelled its ashes (and lugged them to the street), been enslaved to its hourly needs, learned to bank the fire so it would last the night—no one who has not coped with these mystical rites has experienced life fully.

To see the fire through the night you turned the chimney flue almost shut. You shoveled in a good helping of coal, but not so much that you began to smell coal gas. You left the door slightly ajar. If your fire got going too successfully, the boiler which sent steam to the radiators throughout the house was liable to blow off, filling the cellar with billowing clouds of steam. It was a terrifying experience the first time, and only a little less scary thereafter, although it was essentially harmless. It left the cellar damp and dank, with the peculiar smell steam has.

We had a succession of part-time hired men, whose main worry was the furnace. But Jack Convery and Fred White were both subject to "brewer's flu," as Robert Mitchum liked to call the hangovers that make it hard to get started in the morning. I would be dispatched, shivering, to see if I could rouse Jack or Fred at home, an assignment I hated, being uncommonly shy and unassertive.

Fred, watery-eyed but cheerful, would plop in his false teeth (the first I'd ever seen; I asked him to repeat the process over and over again, so I could watch better) and trudge from his tiny house beside the Glen Creek to our place.

Jack Convery was less cheerful, a devoutly sour pessimist who warned me that all the electricity pouring into my ears from listening to the radio would kill me before I reached manhood. He often talked about moving away to Rochester where he would get to see all the pretty girls, of whom there were thousands, he told me. Jack, a bachelor in his late fifties, lived with two maiden sisters, who did dressmaking, and his brother Steve, who was a house painter. Jack never did make it to Rochester.

The attic of our house could only be reached through a trap-door from atop a tall stepladder. My fear of heights began when I was very young, so I never got into the attic. It remained, as in some ways it still does, a tantalizing mystery that was probably full of treasure as well as dust. The only treasure that was ac-

45

tually found up there was a Civil War sword that had belonged to Captain Larrowe, whose daughter was an elderly friend of the family I called Aunt Fan. Joe Eade, another of our hired men, discovered the sword in its worn leather scabbard one afternoon when he was checking for leaks in the roof. I tried to sharpen and to polish the sword but couldn't do either and very shortly it mysteriously disappeared. I think Mother was afraid I might impale myself and simply wanted to get it out of the house. Where it went I've no idea.

The latterday treasures I might have hoped for were letters and photographs, but if there were any there they have long vanished.

My mother had employed Fred and Jack and Joe to tend the furnace and do the heavy chores because from almost the earliest days I can remember we were a fatherless household. Marriages don't fall apart tidily, and my father had not so much disappeared as faded out like the end of a movie scene. I find it almost impossible to conjure up memories of him in the Hammondsport house. My parents separated permanently when I was about six and were divorced when I was nine.

A half-century later divorce is so frequent at every level of society and in every state of the Union that it is difficult to convey the impact—in a small town in the thirties—of having one's parents divorce.

I never felt the guilt that children are supposed to feel. I was certain that my brother and I were not responsible for the break-up of the marriage. Aside from a little noise early on Sunday mornings, we were fairly orderly children, not given to tantrums, running away or setting things on fire. The worst that could be said of us was that our presence had failed to hold the marriage together, as children are alleged to do. But at the time it seemed to me that guilt was all I *was* spared. I felt more than a little bit ashamed, as if something had happened in my family that did not happen in nice families and was unacceptable.

For a few months in 1932 and early 1933, while we were still

46

An outing on Keuka Lake: the author, younger brother Joe, and their mother. The identity and ownership of the dog are unknown.

a family, we had moved to Philadelphia and taken an apartment in Germantown. What I had always understood was that my father was simply attempting to sell sacramental wine from parish to parish. That was legal in those days and the story may have been true, but it may also have been a kind of cover story. Years later my cousin Tony Doherty told me that my father was actually making what you might call bathtub champagne from house to house. For a fee he taught well-to-do clients how to turn grape juice into sparkling wine. He even supplied labels (Mumm's) and lead-foil hoods. Tony found a small trove of them in the Champlin family home and passed a few on to me as mementos.

But I then knew none of that, and I have only such random memories as the angry commands from the bedroom to be quiet on those Sunday mornings in Germantown, and the look of his three-piece brass safety razor and his Eau de Pinaud hair tonic (he lost most of his hair early, despite the Eau), and his amusement the time I woke up with bubble gum in my hair.

Back in Hammondsport, and even before the formal separation, I had been teased about my absent father.

"When's your father coming home, Charles?" a particularly malevolent older boy asked me every time he saw me.

"He's away on business a lot," I remember saying, trying not to let him know that I knew or suspected the real truth, or that he had hit me where it hurt a lot. Small-town children do not have a monopoly on small cruelties, but they perform them very well.

One night when I was nine and reading in bed (an early habit) my mother came upstairs with a copy of the Corning *Leader* and said we might read it together—an odd and unprecedented suggestion. She quickly found her way to a small boxed item on an inside page, slugged "Special to the *Leader*." It reported that she had been granted a divorce from my father. It was an awkward and painful moment for both of us and I thought it was a curious and oblique way to break the news, but in those circumstances no way is better or worse than another.

Now that the divorce had been reported in the newspaper I had no alibis left about my absent father. I felt diminished as well as bereft; demoted and in some way cast out and isolated. As I remember, there was only one other boy in Miss Marian Hamilton's third grade class whose parents had also been divorced. He had never been a close pal, although we went to each other's birthday parties and he had a Lionel train spread of great size, complication and interest. Now I saw the two of us as fellow sufferers, tossing together in the emotional storms, and I tried to be better friends with him. But we never discussed the wound we shared and, although we were always friends, we never became close pals.

The most uncomfortable part of the evening my mother brought me the news of the divorce was that I had very little idea how to comfort her or what to begin to say to her. I would now have to be the man of the house, she said, a theme that was repeated by two grandmothers and assorted aunts and uncles over the next several weeks. It was like dialogue from a not very good film but I went along because I agreed and because I didn't have much choice. In my darkest moments I felt as if I were being trapped into inescapable good behavior and a joyless early maturity. This was not entirely true. Yet I think that being raised by our mother alone, in circumstances that were difficult for her socially as well as economically, had the effect of foreshortening childhood for both my brother and me.

I imagine most children speculate sooner or later on how they and their lives might have been different if their parents had not been divorced. I've fantasized about it a lot over the years. With my father around, I might have been more of a hand with tools and practical matters; I might have been a chemist, might have gone to a different college, might have ended up in the wine business. I might have been less introspective and more extroverted in my early years, might have spent fewer of my childhood and adolescent hours by myself, reading, and I might not have become a writer. And, then again, given the particular patchwork of genes I have within me, I might have ended up much as I have. I can't imagine being totally happy except as a writer.

Emerson's essay "Compensation" made a great impression on me when I read it in college. It is a philosophical way of saying that things work out, or balance out, and I believe it fervently.

The divorce destroyed the kind of settled comfort and security that the middle-class child accepts as his due along with his first spoonful of cereal. It created in me a real enough but temporary feeling of estrangement from the society around me. (I wouldn't have said it or even thought about it that way as a child, but that's what I felt.) On the other hand (and it is another hand), the divorce probably helped make overachievers of both my brother and me, compulsive makers of lists, efficient users of time, incompetent and uneasy relaxers—two boys consciously or unconsciously determined not to let Mother down or to be the cause of any further disappointment, and carrying the achieving impulse far into later adult life as a habit of hard work whose origins are buried in childhood.

Brother Joe, who is four years younger than I am, has no memory of our father at all, not even the timber of his voice (which I would recognize tomorrow; it was rather low, mellow and confiding). For Joe I'm afraid the immediate main consequence of the divorce was that he suffered from more of my bossy attention than he would have had to otherwise. I was not then an ideal older brother, and we fought a good deal.

In fact the childe Charles I see in memory's eye is not unmitigatedly wonderful. Standing aside from him as best I can, I find he tends to role-play or to over-play at being the perfect child, neat, well-mannered and straight-A conscientious. (My grandmother Masson used to say that Joe couldn't stay clean for two minutes, and I couldn't get dirty.)

But childe Charles is also capable of temper and bad deeds. The he that I was also grew up thin and pale and was embarrassed about it. He was afraid of heights and humiliated about it. He was unathletic (Joe inherited the physical skills for both of us). He was bookish and given to inner panic. He was very shy, but outgrew it. He took his role as the little man of the house very seriously, probably too seriously. Meeting him again I might not entirely dislike him, but I would probably want to shake him and tell him to go outside and play.

At the age of eight, the author's brother Joe posed in the vineyard behind the Pleasant Valley Wine Company. Joe is now Monsignor Joseph Champlin of Camillus, New York. *Photograph by Phyllis Keyes*

Family Ties

You would have said that my parents' marriage was made in heaven, that the joining together of those two handsome and popular young people, Malburn Champlin, universally known as Kid, and Katherine (Kitty) Masson had a sort of dynastic inevitability. The Champlins and the Massons had been involved in the ownership and direction of the Pleasant Valley Wine Company since the 1860s, and Kid and Kitty represented the third generation of the families but the first matrimonial link between them.

But if marriages are made in heaven, they are consummated for better and for worse on earth. And it has seemed to me as I've thought about the matter in later years that the times, the town, and the prevalence of family had all contributed to the swift destruction of the marriage.

The two families could hardly have been more different. The Champlins have been English and Protestant: merchants, hunters, fishers, party-givers, celebrators of life, a bit indulgent now and again. My great-uncle Harry Champlin, who died the year I was born, raised race horses and had his own track in Pleasant Valley.

My mother's family, the Massons, were French and German Catholics: hard-working and conservative artisans, thrifty, undemonstrative, strict in their observances, home-centered.

The original Charles Davenport Champlin, my great-grand-

The first Charles D. Champlin

father, had come to Hammondsport from downstate New York when he was sixteen to clerk in his cousin's canal warehouse. Those were the days when Hammondsport was still a busy port, shipping wheat and wool up the lake to Penn Yan and ultimately to New York. In 1860 when the local growers discovered they were growing more grapes than they could sell for table use and decided to start a winery, C. D., who was by then a prosperous farmer and grower himself, became the prime mover and was named secretary. The Hammondsport and Pleasant Valley Wine Company was licensed as U.S. Bonded Winery No. 1, as it still is. The "Hammondsport" was dropped a year later.

Meanwhile, another of my great-grandfathers, Jules Masson, who was born in the tiny village of Marnoz, France, in the Burgundy wine country, had come to the United States to be a winemaker for the Longworth family in Cincinnati. One of the family legends (or a family truth which I can no longer verify) is that Jules and his cousin Joseph landed at New Orleans and took a steamer up the river, pausing in Mississippi long enough to learn some rudimentary English at a grade school before proceeding on to Cincinnati in 1852. There the cousins married sisters, Catherine and Appollonia Reinhardt, who had come from Niederkirchen, Germany.

That scourge of grapes, the blight called *phylloxera*, invaded the Longworth vineyards. By 1869 production had stopped and Jules and Joseph headed east to join the newly-born wine industry at Hammondsport. Joseph, always known as J. D. Masson, became a vineyardist with a big spread that began on the hilltop overlooking the lake five miles north of Hammondsport and ran down to the lake itself. Jules became the works manager and winemaker at the Pleasant Valley Wine Company. (By another family tradition, Jules was the first professional champagne maker in the United States.) I have photographs of Jules, a stout and rather formidable figure in a vested black suit and derby hat, posed with the winery work force on a day in what I calculate was the 1880s. One of his sons, my grandfather, wearing a moustache but looking youthfully pale and thin, stands in the back row. In another photograph Jules poses with his coat off beside a team of horses and a wagon being used to excavate the shale hillside to create more cellars for the winery. By then Jules's champagnes had taken gold medals at European expositions.

54

Standing before the original stone entrance to the Pleasant Valley Wine Company, Jules Masson, the winemaker and works superintendent, wearing a derby hat, posed with the winery employees about a century ago. Two of his sons were on the staff: Arthur, in the center with his arms folded, and Leon, with only his head visible in the back row eighth from the right.

Three of Jules's sons, Arthur, who died young, Leon, my grandfather, and Great-uncle Victor, who was also a winemaker, worked at PV at various times. C. D. Champlin's two sons, Harry and C. A., also worked at the winery. C. A.'s sons were

Hewing the winery's cellars out of the shale cliffs was a monumental job in horse-and-wagon, hand-powered times. Jules Masson, in vest and shirtsleeves, hat in hand, oversees the work. The year was 1891.

my father Malburn and my Uncle Charlie, who was the last of the Champlins to run PV.

My father's name in full was Francis Malburn Champlin, but he never used the Francis. Inside and outside the family he was called Kid, not because he was tough as in boxers named Kid but because he was smooth as in kid gloves. He was relatively short, trim, dapper, and very handsome, with a radio announcer's mellow voice. He attended Mercersburg Academy and Princeton, in those pre-Prohibition days when the winery was prospering. He also studied engineering at Michigan, and after the war, when he served in Naval Intelligence, he worked for a time at Grumman Aircraft on Long Island. Years later when I wrote a column about my father, I heard from an elderly man who had been at Grumman with him—they were developing the altimeter—that he'd been a good engineer. Year by year in the half-century since he died I've learned more about my father and come to like him better.

My mother was a beautiful woman, with black hair and dark brown eyes. The photographs I have of her as a young girl reveal that she was a beautiful child, with a round face and a beguiling smile. I have a series of photographs taken in 1914 when she was sixteen and had been chosen to christen the mahogany-hulled flying boat *America* which Glenn Curtiss had built for the department store magnate Rodman Wanamaker and which Wanamaker hoped to fly to England. (The outbreak of war prevented the attempt.) My mother, wearing a long white ball dress, recited a poem she had written for the occasion and swung the bottle of Great Western champagne. It was supposed to hit an iron frame protecting the fragile hull. It bounced back. She swung again. It bounced back. A young Navy lieutenant stepped forward and swung it by the neck. It broke, splashing them both.

She played the piano unusually well and, to my later delight, could sight-read sheet music effortlessly. Her preferences were for Chopin and Beethoven. For years she was the organist at St. Gabriel's Church, rising without complaint for a seven o'clock High Mass on a weekday. Occasionally, if no one else in the choir could make it, she became the singer as well. She had a pleasant contralto voice.

She went to Vassar in the Class of '22 and used to tell me about crossing the frozen Hudson in horse-drawn sleighs to attend dances at West Point. Some of the cadets she danced with then were generals in the news during World War II. She majored

The matriarch of the Masson family, Grandmother Catherine Reinhardt Masson, was the honored guest at a 1903 luncheon at the "farm," the vineyard home of Joseph D. Masson. His son, Linn, who ran a hardware store in Hammondsport, stands at the right. The little girl is my mother, aged five. Her father smokes a cigar at the other end of the table. Uncle Victor, the family photographer, took the picture.

in chemistry, imagining that she might herself work in the winery. But by the time she graduated, Prohibition had begun and Pleasant Valley was effectively shut down. My father was managing the Champlin family farm, which Sam Baker had started in 1794.

Standing on a makeshift platform, the author's mother, Katherine, a sixteen-year-old schoolgirl, recites a poem at the dedication of Rodman Wanamaker's airship *America* in 1914. Glenn Hammond Curtiss, in a cloth cap, stands at her right. A Navy lieutenant, in civilian clothes, is at left. Holding flowers at right is the author's uncle, W. E. (Gink) Doherty, a pioneer pilot. The mahogany-hulled *America* was designed to fly the Atlantic.

The honeymoon, Mother once told me, had had to be delayed until the asparagus was harvested.

The Roaring Twenties were beginning to roar and I've always

thought that my parents, my father especially, would have fit nicely into a novel by Scott Fitzgerald or, even more likely, by John O'Hara. He was convivial and well-liked. He'd taken violin lessons, but had taught himself to play the piano, which he played wherever there was one. That included the Keuka Yacht Club, the Glenwood Club and, according to my disapproving grandmother Masson, any number of speakeasies in the Finger Lake territory. He was a good cook, although my mother once complained that he used ten pans to make one sauce and never washed any. At one moment, just before Prohibition ended, my father created a French dressing, using some wine vinegar that had accumulated during the dry years. The winery was going to market it and I remember finding some cartons of cruet-shaped bottles in our cellar. But Repeal came along before the dressing went on sale. My cousin Tony says it was wonderful and he's sorry the formula disappeared.

I have a copy of the program of a minstrel show given by the town chapter of the Fraternal Order of Redmen at Hammondsport High School in December 1924. My father, I see, was one of the end men. I suspect that he was a musician-entertainer at heart but pinioned by family tradition and later by wife and children. He was made vice-president of the winery in 1926 when it was for all practical purposes closed but was trying to stay alive in anticipation of the eventual end of Prohibition. After 1933, when Repeal was voted at last, Kid became chief chemist and winemaker at PV. He published at least one paper on industrial aspects of winemaking in the *Journal of the American Chemical Society*. Even when he was no longer living at home and after the divorce, I would go up to the winery, wander through the shadowy, cobwebby catacomb cellars, watching the champagne-making and ending up in my father's laboratory, with its mixed smells of wine and Bunsen burners.

My father naturally did not get good reviews from my mother's mother, Nano Masson. "We never knew where he was, not even the night your brother was born," my grandmother told me more than once when I was a teenager. My father had evidently been off playing the piano somewhere. I had taken up the cornet myself in those days and my grandmother may have been trying to put any such scandalous ideas out of my head from the start. She knew well enough that a cornet could get a person into mischief, too.

It has struck me over the years, remembering those conversations with my grandmother, that there must have been an awful lot of family for my parents to contend with. The Champlin family house where my father was born (and died) was just across the street from ours, and Nano's house, where my mother was born, was just around the corner, hardly two blocks away. I think they could have used a little time away from everybody but themselves. But only my father succeeded—if he did.

Pondering it all—the family pressures, the difference in family life styles, the closeness of the community with its everlasting scrutiny, the expectations from a marriage made in heaven, the economic uncertainties caused by Prohibition (which took much of the Champlin livelihood even while it fueled the national taste for a free-living life style)—I have no trouble understanding why the marriage failed. And I've never doubted that there were two victims and no villain.

Kid Champlin was distinctly not an untarnished hero, and my grandmother was not wrong to be furious at his affection for low companions and unlisted saloons. There was some reason to worry that the Champlins were going to re-enact the old prophecy about shirt-sleeves to shirt-sleeves in three generations, although Uncle Charlie restored the winery expertly and short-circuited the prophecy. Yet I think of the rectitude into which my father married, and the disappointment of harvesting asparagus while the champagne waited to be made, and the yearning to make music and be the life of the party, any party, and I understand if I can't condone. In a way I wish Philadelphia had worked. It might have made a difference, but those months were part of the economic problems which further bedeviled the marriage and I judge there was not much left of it when we trailed back to Hammondsport as the banks began to close.

Not long after the divorce my father was briefly remarried, to a woman who worked on a small daily paper in the area. I was invited across the street to the Champlin house to meet her not long after the wedding. I was uncomfortable and unhappy and prickly with feelings of disloyalty to Mother. Like most people who don't know how to deal with children, my father's new wife treated me like a large baby with diminished mental capacities. She asked me to sit on her lap, which I was at least five years too old to do, and she gave me a large, smeary kiss that left my cheek looking wounded.

The marriage didn't last long. Not much after that I heard that my father was sick (he had cancer) and was living by himself in a rooming house across the street from the Steuben County fairgrounds in Bath. Someone, possibly my grandmother, pointed out the house to me one day as we drove by. In those days I was riding my bicycle up to Bath on Saturday mornings to take a cornet lesson, and one Saturday I went to the boarding house and asked to see my father.

He came downstairs in an old brown bathrobe, looking small and frail but still quite handsome. He sat on the piano stool in the parlor while we talked. He asked about my grades and the cornet and about my brother and our mother. I felt he was touched and pleased that I had come to see him, and he said we would have to see each other again soon, but we never did.

He died on Christmas Day in 1938 when I was twelve, in his mother's house across the street. My mother went over to pay her respects and then came home and ran upstairs to the bedroom and closed the door. My brother remembers that she had us kneel down and say a prayer for him but I think that that was later, when she had composed herself. None of us went to the funeral, and I regret it.

As it had been when she broke the news of the divorce, it was hard to know what to say or do to comfort her. (I felt very sorry for my father but I couldn't make myself cry.) So I did all I could think to do, which was go down and stoke up the furnace and get the radiators thumping and whistling.

In the peculiar but understandable way these things happen I have come to know my father better and better as my own life has proceeded. I don't have much more information about him, but I have come to detect more of him in me. Intending no sentimentality at all, I think we would have gotten along very well if we had had more time to get acquainted. Nano Masson would have been distressed to hear it, but I do think he and I are much alike, even though I can't play the piano.

The truth is that I sometimes now study myself in a kind of Mendelian mirror, or under the light of what we now know about DNA and all that. I speculate on the fall of genes from the Champlin and Masson sides of me (a real Yin and Yang split as we might also say these days). It is interesting, genetically, that my brother Joe inherited my mother's coloring (dark brown eyes and hair) and her and the Massons' strong and serene Catholic faith. I detect that there are within me strong traces of the mundane Masson virtues of hard work and thrift and tidiness (or at least the yearning for tidiness), along with a strong feeling of kinship with most things European and French especially. But I note as well my hazel eyes and light brown hair, as once it was, and a certain raffish *joie de vivre* that I know is the Champlin legacy. The two divergent family strains have set up some real dynamic tensions within me. But, as Charles Atlas might have predicted, I think I'm the stronger for them. And so, out of all these considerations of the past, I end up a bit less puzzled about the I who am I.

It may be, as Norman Cousins argues, that immortality is not a kind of comfortable rest home in which to spend eternity, but rather that it is the life-chain itself, in which we are the momentary link between past and future, joined to both. That kind of continuity was easier to see and feel in the comparatively changeless Hammondsport of the 1930s. A century's worth of history seemed just around the corner, the future was playing with toy cars in the back yard, and there was family all over town to remind you of the chain of which you were a part.

Grandmothers

The Denver poet and essayist Thomas Hornsby Ferril, who was born in 1896, told me once that when he was a boy you could still fairly describe the West as a land without grandmothers. The settling of the frontier was still so recent that families had not had time to extend themselves to a third generation.

Even if this was not quite literally true, it was an arresting and poetic image for a young civilization. As Tom was saying it, I couldn't help thinking that it was doubly telling, because grandmothers have their own well-earned image as the settling, stabilizing influences who hold families together in adversity and who lend a hand with the grandchildren when the parents can't.

(The late comedian Sam Levenson once explained why grandparents and grandchildren get along so well. It is because they have a common enemy, he said.)

I was shortchanged on grandfathers. My paternal grandfather died nine years before I was born and my mother's father, whom we called Baba, died when I was only four. The aroma of cigar smoke brings him back to me, along with a sort of composite memory of sitting on his lap, playing with the steering wheel of the car while we waited for the 5:10 to Buffalo to come steaming into the DL&W depot in Bath. As a special treat he would drive me to the station to see the train. The huge steam engine was thrilling and terrifying in about equal parts. When it had safely stopped we would get out and stand on the platform. My grandfather knew one of the conductors, Mr. Funk, who had relatives in Hammondsport. I thought that knowing a conductor was more awesome than knowing the president. Mr. Funk in his visored hat and his blue uniform with the silver buttons once shook hands with me, very solemnly.

If I ran out of grandfathers all too fast, my grandmothers stayed with me for quite some time. My father's mother I called Nano Pete, to distinguish her from my mother's mother, whom I called just Nano. Nano Pete was the grandmother also of my cousin and exact contemporary Pete Doherty, and thus became Nano Pete. As such nicknames will, "Nano Pete" became widely used in the family. Around Hammondsport she was known slightly more formally as Mrs. C. A., the widow of Charles Addison Champlin, one of the sons of the original C. D. Her maiden name was Georgia Malburn (although I can't remember anyone using the Georgia). Her father was Francis Malburn, of whom I know nothing. Her mother was Helen MacDowell. The MacDowells were an early Colorado family, a fact I wish I had known when I lived in Denver in the early 1950s.

Nano Pete was short, wiry, and strong-willed, a feisty and original spirit who wore a velvet choker and white tennis shoes, often at the same time. To draw near her when she was troweling away was to risk being pressed into service, even if you had only come by to say hello. I found her intimidating because she was direct and outspoken and never seemed to notice whether you were a child or an adult. You had the feeling that she would have said what was on her mind either way. I loved that about her; it was different from the schoolteacherish niceness, which was pleasant enough in its own way, of my Masson maiden aunts. By the time I knew her, her hair was already white but she had fierce black eyebrows. I think of her wearing cotton work gloves and kneeling, trowel in hand, commanding the flowers to grow and prosper.

Her house was diagonally across Lake Street from ours, so

that despite my parents' divorce I always saw a good deal of her. Her daughter, my father's sister Gladys (called Aunt Tommy for reasons lost to memory) had married a colorful pioneer aviator named William Elwood (Gink) Doherty and they and their sons Tony, Duane, and Pete lived in the big yellow house as well. There was a wonderful masculine vitality to the establishment—Nano Pete was not unfeminine but she had a rather deep and crackling voice that rang with authority. The boys hunted, fished, swam and dove like seals, climbed waterfalls and trees, kept hawks, rode motorcycles. It was the farthest possible cry from the Masson entourage, which was dominated by rather sedate widows and spinsters. I was both drawn to and slightly overawed by the Doherty cousins and by Nano Pete, in whose presence I somehow felt bookish and inept (although she was herself a great reader).

Uncle Gink, a dashing raconteur, had flown many of Glenn Curtiss's early experimental planes. When Curtiss, as part of his long legal battle with the Wright Brothers, had Professor Samuel Pierpont Langley's plane fished out of the Potomac (into which it sank after an unsuccessful launch) and reconditioned it, it was Uncle Gink who flew it off the waters of Lake Keuka. Gink's success did not in the end help Curtiss's law suit, because the plane was not allowed in evidence, but the flight became a piece of aviation history anyway.

There are always relatives you wish you had known longer and had had the maturity and the opportunity—or the courage—to ask more about their early lives. Nano Pete died in 1943, the year after I left Hammondsport, and I regret very keenly the questions I never got to ask her or for that matter to ask her son, my father.

I know more about Nancy Eugenia Amsden White Wheeler Masson, my mother's mother, and about her difficult childhood. In maturity she too was short, but tending toward a buxom plumpness. She devoted her life to being wife, mother, and grandmother. She had been raised in the Episcopal Church but, having married into the very Roman Catholic Masson family, she saw

Glenn Hammond Curtiss, in shirtsleeves third from right,
stands before Professor Samuel Pierpont Langley's aeroplane, to be flown by W. E. (Gink) Doherty, who is at right.
The year is 1914. *Courtesy Glenn H. Curtiss Museum of Local History*

to it that Mother was as devout and observant a Catholic as the
Massons could possibly have hoped for. But, partly as a gesture
of her own independence—or so I've always thought—Nano did
not become a convert and remained a staunch Protestant. Dec-
orating the altar each Sunday at St. James's Episcopal Church
was one of the few interests she had outside her family.

She was a wonderful cook and her coconut cake, made from
scratch with the coconut shaved in the kitchen, was one of the
most glorious ways to engulf calories I've ever known. In her last
years, when she was in very fragile health, she drove my mother
crazy by slipping out of bed and starting to make another co-

conut cake, as proof that she had not lost her independence or her ability to contribute to the household. I found it very touching, although at least once she collapsed as she was mixing the cake, and required more care than before. ("I never *intended* to be old," she told me angrily one of the last times I saw her.)

Nano played bridge frequently and well and read in quantity the romantic novels of Faith Baldwin and other writers in the genre. She had a piercing, warbling trill that she used to summon my brother and me (and I presume Mother before us) in to meals or back to the car if we were off on picnics. The shrill trill could be heard for blocks, and if by chance we didn't hear it the neighbors would, and would report, "Charles, your grandmother is calling you." It was a bit humiliating, and very effective.

But all that was years later. Nano was born in Watkins Glen, New York, in 1873 as Nannie or Nancy Eugenia Amsden, the daughter of Marietta C. White and Eugene Amsden. The senior Whites ran The Mountain Home hotel in Watkins Glen and later moved to Cohocton, New York, and ran a hotel in Bath. Amsden turned out to be a bounder who deserted his wife and child when my grandmother was only two months old. I have a certified copy, in a neat hand, of Marietta's divorce decree, granted on grounds of Amsden's adultery, in 1879. (Interestingly, the decree allowed Marietta to marry again, although she never did, but forbade Amsden to marry again in Marietta's lifetime.) Marietta resumed her maiden name and my grandmother called herself Nannie White. Marietta died in 1883 when Nano was only ten, and she went to Hammondsport to live with her uncle, Monroe Wheeler, a lawyer and later for twelve years a surrogate court judge. His wife Emma was Marietta White's sister. In 1889 the Wheelers formally adopted Nano. I have a carbon copy of the adoption papers, with a sweet codicil giving the consent of the child, then fifteen, to the adoption. "I know of no reason why I will not if adopted live there pleasantly and happily & be treated well." It is signed Nancy E. Amsden, her legal name, although she then became Nancy Wheeler.

All that is now a century and more ago, and a century is a respectable piece of time. Nano remembered her mother telling of the family moving from one place to another by covered wagon. That memory, and the defection of her father, a mysterious figure she never heard anything of again, have always seemed to me to be illustrations from the larger history of the country—indicative of a raw time when the towns and cities were thickening but neither the society nor the men and women who composed it had settled into patterns. It was a time that was ending. Nano, having done her own early traveling in horse-drawn buggies, lived to watch television.

Judge Wheeler and his wife had two sons of their own, Sayre and Rumsey. They lived in a large frame house on upper Lake Street toward the wineries. It had previously been called The Erie House and was built, my grandmother said, by the Erie Railroad for one of its managers, possibly in the brief time when the Erie owned the Bath and Hammondsport Railroad. There my grandmother finished her growing up and there she met my grandfather, Leon Joseph Masson. They were married in 1896 when she was not quite twenty-three. My mother, their only child, Katherine Marietta Masson, was born in 1898 on Washington's birthday.

In the years after my grandfather died in 1930, Nano began spending a few weeks each winter in Bradenton, Florida, at the Robert Whitney Hotel, which for a few winters also accommodated some or all of the St. Louis Cardinals, who did their spring training in town. I was by then a baseball zealot. The Rochester Red Wings, the nearest triple-A ball club, were a Cardinal farm club in those years, so I became (and have remained) a Cardinal fan.

My grandmother, who did not know a bunt from a bleacher, brought me a ball signed by all of the 1934 Gas House gang, including Pepper Martin, Rip Collins, manager Frankie Frisch and Dizzy Dean and his brother Paul. She cannot possibly have appreciated quite what a treasure she gave to an eight-year-old grandson. I still have the ball and the signatures are legible beneath the protective varnish Uncle Victor put on it.

My grandmother reported that she regularly played bridge at the hotel with some of the players' wives. My mind boggled when I heard this, because Nano had almost no idea what legendary figures those husbands already were. "I was partnered quite often with a Mrs. Dean," my grandmother said when she came back to Hammondsport early in 1935. "Awfully good bridge player but such *language*!" I asked if it was Dizzy or Paul's wife. "I think he's a pitcher," my grandmother said, which was no help at all.

When I knew more of Nano's childhood I understood why she felt so vehemently about my father's carryings-on. It was rooted in her own father's abandonment of her mother and the insecurities it created in my grandmother's early life. The situations were hardly comparable. Eugene Amsden simply vanished; my father, even after the divorce, was accessible to us. My mother was, I think, able to be more understanding of my father than my grandmother chose to be. As long as she lived and whatever she may have felt, Mother never spoke badly of my father to Joe and me. It is one of the innumerable things I admired about her.

In the great tradition of grandmothers, Nano was the back-up to our fatherless household. She lived in the house she and L. J. had built at 13 Vine Street, opposite the big Jules Masson place and barely two blocks from our house. We went there often for meals, she was our chauffeur (we had no car), and I frequently went over to play cards or Pick-Up-Sticks with her. I stayed with her when I had whooping cough at age five or six and I did my first serious radio listening on a big Philco console she had. One of those images that float up unbidden from childhood is in fact of being silenced while the adults hovered around her radio for the latest news on the kidnapping of the Charles Lindbergh baby.

I think often of Tom Ferril's description of the land without grandmothers and I have no difficulty understanding everything that he meant. The territory lacked that ultimate of all comforts, the grandmothers, with all their wisdom, kindness, and unselfish support. I had only to look at Hammondsport to realize how bereft I would have been without that extended family and my own set of grandmothers. At the very least, life would have been far less interesting. I wouldn't have known that Mrs. Dizzy Dean was a good bridge player.

Victor and the Girls

The relatives I saw most of when I was young—the strongest shaping influences in the family, after my mother—were my mother's mother, Nano Masson, and Uncle Victor Emanuel Masson and his three spinster sisters, Aunt Julie, Aunt Tillie, and Aunt Josie—Julia, Matilda, and Josephine as they were christened. He was actually my great-uncle and they were great-aunts, four of the eight children whom the patriarch and matriarch of the family, Jules Masson and his wife Catherine Reinhardt, had raised in the big yellow house on Vine Street. A fifth child, Uncle Charlie Masson, had moved to California as an electrical engineer in 1912 and returned only occasionally on rare and rather grand visits. He was a friend and I think a neighbor of Shirley Temple's parents and said he had bounced her on his knee when she was a baby. My grandfather, L. J. Masson, and two other of Jules's children were dead by the time I was old enough to know anything about anything.

Jules had built the house in the 1870s and added a huge two-story barn behind it. The barn had stables, quarters for a coachman in the days when they had horses, and a large potting shed. There were brick-edged rose gardens beside the gravel driveway to the barn and a long bed of tulips next to the wrought iron fence that faced on Vine Street. Until Uncle Victor died in 1945, he and a hired man tended a huge vegetable garden which regularly produced the year's first crop of Golden Bantam corn.

The patriarch and his brood sat for a family portrait in 1881.
Jules and Catherine Reinhardt Masson had eight children.
The eldest, Leon, born in 1861 in Cincinnati where Jules was
working for the Longworth vineyards, stands at the rear
with his arms folded. The girls, from the left, are Mathilda,
Julia, Emma, and Josephine. Arthur stands behind his father.
Charles, the youngest (born in 1877) and Victor sit in front.
None of the girls married, nor did Uncle Victor.

Over the years Jules and Uncle Victor after him bought the lots
on either side and at the rear of the original site until the property
stretched from Vine Street to Orchard Street at the back and cov-

ered the middle third of the block. There was an apple orchard at the back and a compost heap, taller than a man's head and concealed by a lattice-work frame, that was as large as a garage. And there were what seemed like acres of lawn, wonderful for running and Cowboys and Indians, with plenty of hiding places. For several years, Aunt Tillie organized an Easter egg hunt for the Sunday School children she taught at St. Gabriel's, and Uncle Victor hid the eggs ingeniously, occasionally suspending them from shrubbery branches in little cloth sacks. The whole place was a child's delight. In the front corner of the barn Uncle Victor had a workbench, including a hand-turned wheel for sharpening tools. Once when I was ten or eleven and fancied becoming a radio announcer, Uncle Victor made a microphone for me by fastening two coffee-can lids together, painting them gold and nailing the device atop a broom stick.

Every year, coincidentally about the time the first strawberries were available in the market, Grandma Masson's surviving brother, Uncle Charlie Reinhardt, used to take the Delaware, Lackawanna & Western train up from Paterson, New Jersey, where he was in the silk business, to celebrate his sister's memory on her birthday, June 17. He was a stout figure in a white linen suit with a matching white straw hat and he smoked cigars, to the unspoken displeasure of my great-aunts, who did not smoke. It was a lawn party (it never rained), with strawberries and golden vanilla ice cream and Aunt Julie's *kuchen,* a kind of semi-leavened cake lavishly sprinkled with powdered sugar. I have a photograph of one of the garden parties, taken by Uncle Victor who, along with his other tinkerings, was an early amateur photographer. Later in my own life, when I had had a chance to see the English countryside and something of France and Germany, I realized that Uncle Charlie Reinhardt's garden party could have been located over there as well. It feels now as if it had existed in another place and time. Like the aunts' use of smatterings of French and German at the dinner table I think of it as a conscious attempt to keep alive the family's European heritage.

The house itself was large (to accommodate eight children it had to be) but light, airy and unpretentious. There was a front parlor with a grand piano which Aunt Julie played very well—she had studied at a conservatory in Boston—and where she sang *lieder* in a lovely contralto voice. They had a wind-up Victrola, but the selections were entirely operatic and of less than no interest to me. There was also a radio the size of a refrigerator to catch Lowell Thomas daily and the Metropolitan Opera broadcasts on Saturday afternoons. The living room had a large bay window overlooking the rose gardens. The chair in it was by custom Uncle Victor's and there he sat, ritually reading the *New York Herald Tribune* through his pince-nez (replaced in later years by a more contemporary style with bows).

Off the living room, with sliding doors to enclose it completely, was the bedroom and bath which Grandma Masson occupied in her last years after she had had a paralytic stroke. From some guarded remarks my grandmother made I have the impression that Catherine Reinhardt was a holy terror even before her stroke, and I have suspected that she made life difficult for my grandmother, possibly for daring to take one of her boys away (even if only diagonally across Vine Street) and perhaps for not being Catholic. In the family photographs, Grandma Masson looks like a wisp of a thing, with a will of iron.

The fact that none of their four daughters married and that Uncle Victor remained at home and single to assume the role of *pater familias* after Jules died tells me a lot about the supreme and tethering importance of family in the Masson household. In the European tradition the family was the rock and the constancy, and I can only believe that it was difficult for the sons and daughters to pry loose. My grandmother made some guarded allusions to beaus who got away because they were not Catholic or failed to pass the tests of Jules and Catherine in some other way. Aunt Julie was the loser in these references and, while my grandmother may have over-dramatized the circumstances, it's not hard to believe there were eager suitors; she was the most beautiful of the girls. But they stayed home to care for Grandma until she died, and by then the girls were in their forties.

I call them the girls because my grandmother did. Identifying who was coming to dinner or going on a picnic or to the cottage for a swim, she would say "Victor and the girls." I thought it was funny because to me they seemed wonderful but ancient. Yet I did some calculating recently and realized that when I was ten years old, Aunt Julie was sixty and Uncle Victor, the youngest, only fifty-two—not young but not ancient, either.

Aunt Tillie and Aunt Josie had taught school and Aunt Tillie was a "Miss Masson," although "Miss Chips" would have been as fitting a title to generations who took high school French and German from her. She was the merriest of the family, a story-teller and jokester who loved rhymes and puns.

Uncle Victor had studied chemical engineering at Lehigh on a scholarship from the Lehigh Valley Railroad and followed his father as winemaker at Pleasant Valley. It is another of the family legends, also possibly true, that Uncle Victor put the fermenting of champagne, until then somewhat haphazard, on a scientific basis. (It is probably a myth that in earlier days they waited until a quarter of the bottles had exploded from too much pressure before deciding the fermentation was complete and the bottles could be recorked.) Later he was a winemaking consultant to Taylor and some other American wineries, including Cook's. When the last of the Massons, Aunt Josie, died in 1955 and the house was emptied and sold, I inherited stacks of photograph albums and stereopticon slides Uncle Victor had made himself, going back to his undergraduate days at Lehigh. He had the meticulousness of the true scientist. Each print was dated and identified in his small, neat hand. I have also inherited a few gallons of a very sweet, Tokay-like dessert wine Uncle Victor made. It too was labeled in his small, neat hand, but it had been stored in a damp cellar and the date had become illegible. It cannot be less than fifty years old, and it is quite possible it was made before World War I. It has kept as well as it has because of its high sugar

The Masson girls posed for their brother Victor's camera on a Sunday afternoon, September 3, 1893. Tillie, in front, is flanked by Julie and Josie, with solemn Emma at right and a friend peeking over Aunt Tillie's shoulder.

content; it is almost as heavy as syrup. I have a sip now and again to stir the echoes and be sure it is still OK.

Life with the Massons was not as worldly and outgoing as it was in the Champlin households, but it was not grim and cheerless either. Victor and the girls loved to go on picnics to the shady glens around Hammondsport, and I must say I never minded going along. There were rock pools to play in and Aunt Julie's sandwiches were terrific. In the tidy division of labors in the Masson house, she did the cooking and Tillie and Josie saw to the table and the housecleaning. Uncle Victor ran the household accounts from his study directly over the living room. It had its own bay window overlooking the gardens and glass-doored bookcases on the other walls. To this day, if I were to design a home office from scratch, I would make it as much like Uncle Victor's study as I could.

In the summer Victor and the girls went up the lake to stay at the cottage J. D. Masson had built at the turn of the century for his dying son Ray, home from California with tuberculosis. In the thirties it was still semi-finished, the studding exposed. It had no electricity or running water, and the outdoor plumbing ("Use Lime Every Time") was a spidery adventure. There was a crank telephone on the wall and a battery radio for Lowell Thomas and Amos and Andy. Joe and I always went to stay with them for a week or so, falling into the pleasant rhythm of regular, simple meals and plenty of time in the rowboat and the water. We also played catch, with a ball that went in the lake so often it was finally hard and heavy as a piece of granite.

To the Massons I expect I owe whatever lingering dream of tidiness in all things that I may have, along with some part of my fondness and admiration for words and matters of the mind, and some leaning toward the culture of Europe. There was a warmth and an orderliness about life on Vine Street that was very appealing. I felt it when I was quite young, even if I didn't know enough to articulate it. The serenity that Uncle Victor and the aunts appeared to find in their faith was also attractive to me, and enviable. The steadfastness of their devotions was almost saintly; it was as if they were religious figures, but out of uniform. (They said the Rosary each night at the cottage, and if Joe and I had gone to bed early we could hear the murmurings from downstairs.)

79

My delightful great-aunts, Julie, Tillie, and Josie, chatted with me on my visit to Hammondsport in the summer of 1949. We sat on the wide and airy side porch. It was the last time I saw the three of them together. The last of the sisters, Aunt Josie, died in 1955 and the house Jules Masson built was sold.

What I can't be sure of now is whether their constancy and their celibacy were presented as a conscious choice for their lives, as it must in religious vocations, or whether by the time I was old enough to know them they had simply resigned themselves to lives as they had been ordained by family tradition. "Tethered as we are by the iron chain of circumstance," Ulysses S. Grant wrote somewhere in his memoirs, and it furnished the title for a book of short stories, *The Iron Chain,* by Edward Newhouse.

The phrase has stuck with me and I think of it when I remember my uncle and my aunts. It is an irony and a sad one that among them all, Jules's and Catherine's eight children produced only three children of their own. That grand and hierarchical family is no more. There are no more Massons, only us collaterals to raise a grateful salute to Victor and the girls, in his sweet Tokay.

Writer at Work

Despite the divorce, both sides of my family remained cordial with each other. (Actually, they had never done any socializing that I remember; their contacts had all been at the professional and business level, at the winery.) And all the aunts and uncles and cousins stayed close to and supportive of my brother, my mother and me. That was the plus side of divorce in a small town, I suppose; there wasn't so much anger as pained regret, with everybody agreeing to make the best of a sad business.

My father's brother, Uncle Charlie Champlin, kept a close eye on us. He occasionally took me along on trips to Rochester, and he introduced me to the malted milk shake. The winery was still struggling to get going again after Prohibition and money was scarce there, too. But Uncle Charlie arranged for Mother to earn money by typing envelopes for the annual reports to stockholders. It was tedious work, which she did on a lumbering old Royal manual typewriter. For days what was customarily her sewing area at the top of the stairs would be white with piles of envelopes, geographically sorted. I typed some of the envelopes myself, beginning a lifelong association with the keyboard and theoretically anyway (I didn't get paid) using it as a source of income for the first time. Later Mother worked in the winery office and then as a teller at the Bank of Hammondsport. Our financial affairs stabilized a little, although at a low level. We never owned a car.

As I think back on it, our economic status in those years was peculiar. The three of us constituted a kind of patch of shabby gentility upon a family fabric that might have seen even better days but that was still relatively intact. I never quite thought of us as poor relatives, but I was never unaware that money was a problem. I wince with shame to remember afternoons when I sided with traveling salesmen who were trying to sell Mother hand-tinted photographs of us boys (she said OK and they were terrible) or a newfangled hair brush. Jules Masson had invested so conservatively and his descendants lived so unostentatiously that even the one-two punch of Prohibition and the stock market crash did not seriously graze them. The families were always there as safety nets, but Mother was determined to prove she could make it on her own and preserve her independence and ours. She accepted work from the winery but allowances from no one, even though my father was in no financial shape to help us.

I still have the small red savings account book my Grandfather Masson opened for me at the Bank of Hammondsport the week I was born. For the first few years the balance kept bouncing down almost to zero. It would sink to five dollars and then inch back up to twenty-five or thirty dollars, seldom higher and seldom for very long. I may be reading too much into the columns of figures (entered in ink, with initials I recognize: EH for Ed Hunter, the president, LK for Loper Keyes, the vice-president, and the others). But it's obvious that Mother used the account as her last resort piggy-bank, to be drawn on when the need was desperate, as when the rent came due. I've kept the account alive all these years, adding a token sum every January as a hostage to my own fates.

As the years went on and in the great American tradition, I did whatever I could to earn pocket money. I peddled the *Saturday Evening Post* and *Ladies Home Journal* and for a brief period I sold Scripto ink and Mentholatum salve from door to door, with uncommonly little success. I delivered handbills (which is the most boring, wearying job ever invented). One summer I created a paper route to the cottages, bicycling three or four miles up one side of the lake, back through Hammondsport and three miles up the other side and back. It was crazy, as anyone could have told me, and on a good day—a very good day—I may have averaged three sales per mile. Also it rained a lot and I imagine most of the papers were bought out of sympathy for the bedraggled fool at the door. But it was good exercise, and if persistence is a virtue it was one I could claim.

All those hours on the bicycle, like the winter hours I spent reading on an ancient wicker chaise-longue in my bedroom, were perfect for developing a fantasy life. For reasons that even now I can't quite account for, the richest and most persistent fantasy I had was of becoming a writer. So far as I'm aware there had never been a writer in the family on either side, although there had been plenty of enthusiastic readers. I didn't know any writers or any aspiring writers. Yet again and again I saw myself sitting at the typewriter, puffing a pipe, withdrawing checks from envelopes, seeing my words in print. I also fantasized about hitting home runs and playing cornet solos of unbelievable brilliance, but those fantasies were so thoroughly unbelievable that I wasted very little time on them.

A friend of mine once asked Robert Frost when he decided he was a poet. Frost said, "My dear, when did you decide you were a beautiful woman?" He meant that there was no conscious decision involved, only a recognition of a truth that was inescapable. I've said, and I think it's true, that your first tip-off that there may be writing in your future comes very early. It is, let's say, a little easier for you than for some of your pals to write those awful thank-you notes at Christmas time for the box of handkerchiefs you'd always wanted (or, as was more likely the case, hadn't). I was a whiz at thank-you notes and I could type long before I was ten. After that I was just following the lines of least resistance.

And so as I stumbled toward adolescence I was already becoming a cliché: the would-be writer whose richest life is led in the imagination, fired by radio, movies, books, pulp magazines, and all that solitude.

Being a writer was its own kind of dream but it never seemed an impossible dream, like meeting Shirley Temple. If you don't have a live-in father as a role model (or even as an anti-role model, a sort of living set of Don'ts), you are freer than most to invent your own role in your head. Some of my adolescent fantasies, including the visions of being a published writer, are as vivid to me now as when I first entertained them. For quite some time I wanted to be thought *inscrutable*—in the manner, it may have been, of Lamont Cranston, who was in reality The Shadow. "Charles Champlin is so *inscrutable*," I wanted to hear people whisper behind my back. *Cool* and *aloof* would have been good, too. I wanted in those days to have a trench coat, so I could walk around, hands in pockets, my collar up, looking cool, aloof *and* inscrutable, and observing people. Writers are unobtrusive observers, noting everything. I wanted to observe. The fact is that I only managed to look bored, sallow, and mopey. Once at a Boy Scout meeting, where it was not easy to look inscrutable anyway, my platoon leader asked me if I was feeling sick.

More romantically, I had fantasies of being someone like Flash Gordon, standing his ground on muscular legs in those space-age Dr. Dentons of his, holding evil at bay. My dreamy plot was that only I could protect the girl, whoever she was, from the danger, whatever it was, and in my recurring fantasy I had my arm around her, keeping the rain off. (This may have been the first manifestation of the lifelong incurable romantic, emerging from the larval stage.)

Later (but not much later; I really was a precocious reader), Flash Gordon faded away and I became Lieutenant Henry, walking back to the hotel in the rain from the hospital where Catherine has died, in Hemingway's *A Farewell to Arms*. The collar of the trench coat is turned up, the inscrutability now only a desperate, tragic weariness.

In real life I did all the normal things. I played endless hours of catch with Joe, trying to master the curve and the knuckleball. We played softball in the backyard and on the diamond behind the old schoolhouse where the Curtiss Museum is now. I became a Boy Scout First Class with two merit badges (Reading and Scholarship); I went to Boy Scout camp (and caught impetigo) and suffered through overnight hikes, when it usually rained. I took piano lessons unsuccessfully from Evangeline B. Perry, the Presbyterian minister's wife. I started a correspondence course in cartooning with the W. L. Evans School of Cartooning in Cleveland, Ohio, becoming pupil L-3954, but abandoned it when I could not master a pen portrait of Theodore Roosevelt. I went swimming at Putnam's Dock at the lakefront on summer afternoons. I learned to take apart and reassemble the New Departure brake on my bicycle (my first and almost my only mechanical triumph). I bought my first suit, a pepper and salt green tweed affair with a belted-in-the-back jacket and two pairs of pants, at Richman Brothers in Elmira.

And I read and read, and read some more, and in those warming fantasies I heard an editor say, "God, this kid is *good*."

Box 175

Unless you lived on one of the Rural Free Delivery routes down the lake or up in the hills, there was no mail delivery in Hammondsport. There isn't, even now. That made the post office the true nerve center and social focus of the town. When I go back in the summertime now I see that to a degree it still is the heart of things, except that people roar up in cars instead of on foot and the visits don't last as long. But in the thirties if you stood around the high writing desk long enough, looking at the Wanted posters and checking out the ink wells and the scratchy stick pens, sooner or later you would see virtually everyone in Hammondsport who could walk.

The mail came down from Bath in a truck twice a day, but the morning mail was the big and important delivery. It contained the first class mail from the New York- and Buffalo-bound trains that stopped at the DL&W depot. When the truck arrived the teller windows would be closed and you could hear the sorting going on inside. By the time the windows opened again, the post office would be crowded. A friend of mine used to say it was so quiet in the part of Iowa where he grew up that you would go ten miles to watch them grease a windmill. In Hammondsport you went to the post office. In the summer if I wasn't peddling newspapers I went to the post office every day. From an early age—about as soon as I got beyond spelling "cat" and "hat," the mail was an important link to the great world for me.

You could get your mail at the General Delivery windows, of course, but like most of the permanent residents we had a box. It seemed more secure and private, but having a box also meant you could get your mail when the windows were closed. For years I could remember the numbers where you set the two little dials to unlock the box. The numbers have now slipped from memory, although I occasionally dream that I am opening Box 175 and finding exactly what I had hoped to find. Finding forgotten caches of money or other treasures is a common dream, I understand, but it's probably significant that my pleasing surprises turn up in the mail box. It is one of the most comforting and reassuring dreams I have.

It always took an act of will to wait until all the mail was up before you opened the box. You could hear letters click against the doors as the clerks tossed them in. You got a postcard-sized pink notice, dog-eared from many uses, if you'd received a parcel too large for the box. There was a small rectangle of glass in the door of the box and you could glimpse the pink card, and if you were expecting something really important the wait was a sweet anguish.

The first things I remember waiting for with a terrible impatience were, of course, the premiums I had ordered from the radio serials I listened to every afternoon. Like millions of American children in the thirties I sent away for rings made out of horseshoe nails from "Tom Mix" and a tin badge with a disc you could spin to make a picture of Tom. There was a secret decoder pin from "Little Orphan Annie" that was indispensible to "Annie" listeners because at the end of each program the announcer would dictate numbers that when decoded spelled out the next plot turn.

It still gives me pause to toss an empty cereal box into the trash. I used to beg for particular brands just to get the box tops; that was the whole point, as it still is. Now it feels curiously wasteful not to need the box top to get something from Jack Armstrong the All-American Boy. The other day I opened a jar of Ovaltine and was astonished not to find a thin aluminum seal beneath the lid. That thin aluminum seal (always described in those words) was what Orphan Annie required from you (plus a dime or a quarter) to obtain whatever premium was going that week. I wish I had any of the premiums now. Their value as collectibles would undoubtedly keep you in Ralston, Wheaties or Ovaltine for months.

One of the revelations that came to me later in life was that I fell in love with the mail when I was very young because the mail was indifferent to my age. I spent the first twenty-five or thirty years of my life wishing I *was* older or at least looked my age or older. (That wish turned upside down soon enough, of course.) But if you could type, as I could quite early in a hunt-peck way, and if you could write reasonably coherent English, whoever got your letter couldn't be sure if you were ten or twenty-two. So, in my impatience to be thought older I hid behind the typewriter and further disguised myself with precociously pompous prose.

I wrote to newspapers, complaining sincerely but angrily about their choice of comic strips. None of these was ever printed or answered that I remember. Maybe my literary disguise was not perfect. But I also wrote away for catalogues whenever they were offered and it used to thrill me to receive a letter from a corporation that assumed I was an adult and said it welcomed my inquiry, looked forward to an early order and assured me of the company's high regard. (Long after the fact I apologize to the corporations for the unnecessary bother I caused them and thank them for the good they did to my spirits.)

Not long after I took up the cornet I got on the mailing list of a company that printed posters—the kind you put in store windows and tack to telephone poles—for dance bands. I hadn't progressed much beyond "My Old Kentucky Home" at that time, but just knowing where I could buy those posters in garish colors and at reasonable prices fed my fantasies in a marvelous way. One mail order purchase I did make was an enormous quan-

The author at age thirteen at Boy Scout camp.

tity of stationery—enormous in relation to my real needs, a thousand each of letterheads and envelopes. (Actually it was a bargain which did not cut deeply into my *Saturday Evening Post* earnings.) They were business-size letterheads that would have been fine for a minor conglomerate. My name, all of it, including the "3rd," was splashed large across the page in a typeface called

Stymie Bold, which has bulbous serifs and carries echoes of Barbary Coast saloons. I wrote the address as "Lake at Orchard Streets," thus greatly elevating the status of the dirt alley beside our house. Letterheads in hand, I sent for ever more catalogues, got on mailing lists and received more letters than Mother did. I entered contests. I wrote to WHAM, a radio station in Rochester, for the autographs of my favorite announcers (not yet called disc jockeys). The station sent them, on a sheet headed, "From the elucidators of WHAM."

It was very upsetting to me when a grown-up looking package would arrive and be sent to my namesake uncle across the valley, perhaps because the cereal company had left off Box 175 or because the clerks, working fast, hadn't bothered to look. Aunt Jessie or Cousin Caroline would call to tell me the package had arrived (they were outside the village limits and on rural delivery) and I would walk or ride my bicycle across the valley a mile or so to my uncle's house to pick it up, feeling slightly foolish. I particularly remember that my Little Orphan Annie Ovaltine Mug went over to Uncle Charlie's, because in my haste to open it when I got home I sliced my right index finger with a kitchen knife so nastily that the scar is still faintly visible. After a while I had written away for so much stuff that I occasionally got mail intended for Uncle Charlie—a sample bag of corks for the winery and a catalogue from a manufacturer of cardboard cartons.

I spent so much time with them that the postal clerks and the postmaster became a further extension of the already extended family I felt Hammondsport was. The postmaster in the thirties, John Richards, a Democrat and a Franklin Roosevelt appointee, was "Jernie" to everyone in town and Uncle Jernie to me, although he was no kin but only one of the innumerable ghost uncles and aunts I had in those days. The most colorful of the clerks was Jack Van Loan, a myopic bachelor with a vast belly. His life's companion was a low-slung dog with an equally vast belly, earned by drinking beer from saucers in the taverns Jack frequented. Jack, a cigarette invariably hanging from the corner of his mouth, peered at you over his glasses, wheezed a lot and walked with a kind of flat-foot, splay-foot shuffle. Jack, trailed by his sway-back hound and trudging down Main Street toward his house where he lived with his mother, was one of the village originals. He was vivid and unique as I remember him, but there must have been something of desperation in a life so narrowly circumscribed, and I think of him now with both affection and sadness.

Minor Swarthout was a handsome and dapper man whose wife, Laura, was a newspaperwoman. Her brief history of Hammondsport is still a useful document. The Swarthouts' son, Joe, was to become president of the Taylor Wine Company, the last of the locals to hold the job after the winery was sold to Coca-Cola. The elder Swarthout was the most reserved of the clerks, but I always thought I detected a hint of amusement in his eyes. On occasion he handed me the radio show premiums, too large for Box 175, with a grave understanding of just how much they meant to me. Louise Eckel must have been the youngest of the clerks, because when I went back to Hammondsport in later years she and Steve Douglass, who followed Jernie Richards as postmaster, were still at the teller windows—familiar faces who reminded me that not all my links to Hammondsport had been cut.

Harold Wood was the clerk I came to know best, because he was for years the Scoutmaster of Troop 18 and I did my first overnight camp-outs, pitched my first pup tent and did my first campfire cooking (disastrous) under his patient auspices, in the hills above town or at the head of the lake, which is now called Champlin Beach. Troop 18 could break any drought by scheduling an overnight hike; it was sure to rain.

Harold had been a star athlete at Hammondsport High and he retained always an athlete's lean, trim build. He was unceasingly cheerful, with eyes full of amusement and tolerance, a long and thoughtful nose, and an electric shock of black hair. Harold

and his wife Carol had one son, Reg, who was a year or so older
than I was, a soft, scholarly boy who had inherited none of his
father's athletic skills. When the war came, Reg joined the Infantry and by a twist of fate was shot down over Italy in a troop-
carrying plane. The rustic Scout building alongside the creek is
called the Reginald Wood Memorial to Scouting, a gesture to
both son and father. It seemed to me that if any man and woman
deserved a better break from the fates for all they had contributed
to the world they lived in, it was Harold and Carol Wood. I think
of them now, Carol waiting to restore us with lemonade as Harold and Reg and the rest of Troop 18 stuffed the Woods' barn
with the tons of waste paper that financed the troop for years.

Harold remained the guiding spirit of Scouting in Hammondsport as long as he lived, but it cannot have been the same
for him after Reg died. I stopped to see Harold whenever I got
back to Hammondsport after the war, but I felt that the meetings
were uncomfortable for both of us. Finishing college, marrying,
taking my first job, I was acting out something of what Reg's
uncompleted life might have been, and we both felt it. When I
read in the *Steuben Courier-Advocate* of Harold's death I confess
that I wept, and I could only hope that he knew how much and
how positively he had figured in the lives of so many of us.

The post office as I first visited it was located in a storefront
next door to Clarence Payne's meat market. Later it moved a
block nearer the lake, on the corner where Fay's market had been.
It is still there and so, I have seen, are the old tiers of private
boxes, including Box 175. The chained pens at the high counter
are ballpoints but they don't work much better than the stick
pens did. The Wanted posters still make interesting reading and
I look them over, mostly to have a reason to linger in the post
office and remember how many of my fantasies the mail helped
to feed. In my cornet days, for example, I subscribed for a while
to *Downbeat*. It must have been the only copy of the magazine
that came into town. There were dance band arrangements sta-
pled into it. I didn't know how to play them but I saved them

against the day when I would, although they disappeared before the day came. But I followed the doings of the big bands and the big instrumentalists. Who else in Hammondsport knew what Irving Fazola was up to? One of these years, I told myself, I would be out doing one-night stands with the bands.

Switching fantasies, I answered the advertisements in *Open Road for Boys*, the Boy Scout magazine, for correspondence courses in cartooning. The magazine carried cartoons by amateurs on a special page. I enrolled in the W. L. Evans Course of Cartooning in Cleveland, Ohio. I think I paid five dollars down and was sending one dollar a month toward a total of thirty dollars. I became pupil L-3954 and sent off my tightly-rolled drawings with return postage, and back they would come, tightly re-rolled and now bearing W. L.'s admonitory comments ("You MUST try harder, Charles") and his confident corrections, all in curvilinear flourishes of lavender ink. W. L. had taught Chester Gould and sent him on his way to fame and fortune as the creator of Dick Tracy. But W. L. failed with me, or vice-versa. What ruined me was a pen portrait of Theodore Roosevelt (who I suspect was in office when the course was designed). All I had to do was copy the damned thing. But, although I bought India ink and sent away for all the right pen nibs and even made a preliminary pencil sketch with carbon paper, I couldn't get the portrait right. I had to do it again and again (which meant week after week), with increasingly sharp reprimands from W. L. about my shaky and unconfident pen-work. I finally faced the fact that yet another avenue to fame and fortune was closed to me. I never got to lesson six. I said the heck with it, cut my losses and abandoned the course to concentrate on the cornet, for which I still had some hopes. I was disappointed and somewhat ashamed of my lack of will and sticktoitiveness. But as I went bumping along through my teens, I saw that a lot of life is trial and error. If at first you don't succeed, try failing at something else for a change.

In the long run my stab at cartooning had a life-enriching effect on me. It led me to the *New Yorker,* which then as now

94

printed the best cartoons, as I had discovered looking at copies of the magazine at Uncle Charlie's house. The Park Pharmacy received two newsstand copies of the *New Yorker* every week, and I asked Mr. Hoyt, who ran the store, to put one away for me. It then cost fifteen cents, I think.

By the time my dreams of cartooning fame faded away, I had discovered that the wonderful cartoons were surrounded by even more wonderful words. There were the witty and anonymous Notes and Comments (which I discovered years later were written most often at that time by Wolcott Gibbs and E. B. White). There were stories by James Thurber, John O'Hara, and Irwin Shaw, and the economical and often brilliantly derisive book reviews by Clifton Fadiman. The film critic was John Chapin Mosher and, in a *New Yorker* tradition that lasted until Pauline Kael took over, I don't think he liked the movies very much. (Wolcott Gibbs, who did it for a while, described the movies as aimed at an audience "incapable of reading without moving its lips.")

My flirtation with the cornet lasted decades longer than my attempts at cartooning, although after a while I abandoned any thought that the cornet was anything more than a side pleasure. I was wise enough to know that Bobby Hackett and Jimmy McPartland were unthreatened, to say the least. But the message I kept getting from my links with the great world, activated by my typewriter through Box 175, was that the possibilities of the written word really were immense. The typewriter was mightier for me than the drawing pen, and Box 175 helped me to see that whatever I did with my life it would do well to involve putting words together.

The Gas Station

A few years ago as I watched Barry Levinson's film *Diner* about his young years in Baltimore, I felt a glow of recognition. It wasn't that we had had a diner in Hammondsport. As I remember, the nearest diner was on the far side of Bath, a good ten miles or more away, and that was beyond our turf in those generally carless days.

It was the *idea* of the diner that was immediately familiar: the diner as the place where you congregated with your pals. There was obviously never a village so small or a city so large that it didn't have one or possibly dozens of hangouts like Levinson's diner.

For the small circle to which I attached myself in the Hammondsport of my youth, our gathering place—our diner—was the Atlantic gas station at the monument corner where Lake and Main Streets intersect.

It was in those days a small, white clapboard building hardly larger than a log cabin. There was a main room where the stove was, an adjoining room where the candy and soft drinks (the station's limited menu) were sold, a back room for storage and where, from time to time when the state police looked the other way, there were pinball machines that paid off in nickels. There was also another, smaller back room with a cot, where one of the proprietors used to keep a stash of pre-*Playboy* girlie magazines that became part of my early education.

It was, like all the other hangouts, a multi-purpose place: part sanctuary from the cares of home, school, and unemployment, part gossip center, part rallying point for adventures, part forum for public discussion of serious philosophical issues like sex or Harley-Davidsons vs. Indian motorcycles (a prime topic in the thirties).

There were other hangouts in Hammondsport—the Carrasas family's Keuka Restaurant, Smellie's Drug Store, the park in summer, and some if not all of the other gas stations and garages in town. I suppose part of the appeal of the gas stations was that you could hang around longer without having to buy anything. But the big thing was the obsessive interest in cars themselves. Despite Henry Ford's Model T and the democratizing of car-owning that began in the twenties, the automobile was still tantalizingly out of reach for many families and almost all teenagers in those years when the Depression and I were both young.

A few of my friends had been clever enough to acquire an old hulk and make it run. Gasoline cost as little as twenty cents a gallon (I remember a special sale of five gallons for a dollar) but it was still bought a gallon at a time, maybe two, and there were stories about going up hill in reverse so the cupful of gas left in the tank would run down into the carburetor. Only one of my contemporaries had a new car of his own in high school, and this was because he had been left a trust fund—and had a wonderfully understanding trustee.

So everybody talked cars and watched cars go by, and the fascination with anything that had an internal combustion engine in it was the magic that held the gas house gangs together. The gangs, it is probably necessary to say, were never gangs in the big city sense. There were no rivalries, no crimes large or petty that any of our crowd was ever involved in, no violence. There was also no television to keep us at home, naturally, so the filling station or just the station as we called it functioned as a kind of living theater in which we were all actors. Of a sort.

Hammondsport had an unusually large number of gas stations

and garages for a village of twelve hundred. There were Ben Casterline's Flying A garage and one opposite him that sold bait and ice and Rotary gas, both down at the end of Main Street between the B&H Railroad tracks and the Cold Stream Inlet. Mike Canteloupe's Sinclair station and Sherm Wright's Sunoco garage were on the other side of town, just off the village square by the creek. There were also Drew's Esso garage and Chapman Chevrolet, the last dealership in town, where you could also buy gas. Each of these places had its own shifting population of well-wishers, who hung around to watch grease jobs and talk cars, and maybe pump gas as a favor if the proprietor was elbow-deep in a motor.

But the Atlantic was the most popular spot. It was across the street from the school and, being at the monument corner, it was the most central. Our house was only three doors up Lake Street from the Atlantic, so my acquaintance with it began very early— in first grade, in fact. Newman Worden, the proprietor in those days, sold penny candy and some basic school supplies, and I was a customer for the candy. There were miniature Mr. Good-bars and Butterfingers you could buy for a penny apiece, although none of my children ever believed that this could have been true.

As the years went by and a succession of proprietors followed, I took to hanging around the gas station longer and longer, listening to the talk and lingering over a Nehi chocolate drink and a Clark Bar or a Bunte Tango. I was the youngest of the hangers-on, still in grade school (there being no junior high school in those years) while the others were in high school or already graduated. It was years before I understood some of the jokes that I heard. But I soaked up everything, acquiring bits and pieces of lore that would unquestionably have shocked my mother, or would have shocked her to know that I knew them.

One of the proprietors was subject to what sounded like really terrible romantic problems, involving both unfilled yearnings and cruel rejections. In especially somber moments he would murmur, "The more you know about women, the less you know about women," and I would nod with the others and say, "Yeah, heck," as if I had a glimmering of what he was talking about. It was not only the jokes that I tumbled to the meaning of years later. Another of the proprietors was a sweet, sad man who had never found a second act to match the pride and excitements of his very young days when he had worked for Glenn Curtiss. When Curtiss moved his factory to Buffalo during World War I, George was left behind. He can hardly have been into his twenties, but it was as if his life was all behind him. He was, I realize now, descending into alcoholism very fast, and any one of his days would be marked by successive waves of exuberant storytelling and a wet melancholy. He had that gift of turning fairly ordinary happenings into funny stories that depended on wild exaggeration—the minor skid that became a slewing 360-degree spin, the wife's anger that became a fusillade of pots and pans.

Sometimes on his exultant Saturday nights he would refuse to let any of his friends pay for their gas. "Who's running this wigwam, you or me?" George would shout. His favorite lines came out again and again, as if on automatic pilot, and that was one of them. He also liked to say, "My father's favorite swear word began with 's' and he would use no other." He complained frequently about the very large granite boulder that marks Curtiss's grave in Pleasant Valley Cemetery. "G.H. would be *outraged* if he could see it," the proprietor would say in a low and loyal voice. "He was not fancy. It was not his way."

Did I say the gas station was theater? It surely was, offering a range of moods from farce to the discomfort of watching George in his blurry decline. One summer afternoon a car pulling a small trailer drove into the station's macadam forecourt, and from the car emerged four excruciatingly beautiful young men who walked with a studied grace that was almost balletic. I cannot yet have been twelve and I was not profoundly sophisticated, but I sensed even then that they might have been what were called fairies in some of the improbable jokes told at the station. The

four of them came inside, cool but certainly aware of the astonished gazes of the gang, who were macho to a fault. They bought
Cokes.

They were a team of magazine subscription salesmen, working their way west from New York City, their leader explained.
He demonstrated beautifully manicured, pointed, and polished
fingernails—the better for displaying the pages of magazines, he
said. The team, he went on, was looking for recruits. Perhaps we
knew someone who would like to travel; it was interesting work.

My sophistication was, it needs no saying, less than total. I
thought of one of the gang, not there at the moment, who was
out of school and needed a job and I blurted "Maybe Paul—"
before one of my pals gave me such a sidewinding kick I almost
fell down. "Oh, no, I just remembered he can't leave town," I
said lamely, in two senses.

The salesmen finished their Cokes, without haste, and got
back in the car and drove away. When they had gone, the proprietor, who was that summer an earnest young man from a local
vineyarding family, grabbed a fistful of paper towels and wiped
the door knobs and any other surfaces he thought the visitors
had touched, as if their life-style might turn out to be contagious.
Even then, a half-century before AIDS entered anybody's vocabulary, it seemed like an over-reaction and the proprietor was kidded about it.

It was a long time ago but the scene, like many others from
those days at the station, has played itself over in mind many
times down the decades. I've wondered what the four travellers
talked about in the car after their encounter with the village lads
at the Atlantic, and what mad hopes and desperations put them
on the road into such alien territory on what must have been, on
the face of it, a doomed enterprise. There may have been a hidden
agenda but I could not then have guessed what it was, and I'm
not sure the big guys could have either.

Like Levinson with his Baltimore diner, I can't get the gas
station out of my mind. I try to tell myself the hours I spent at

100

the Atlantic could have been more profitably employed in home-work or chores. But I also tell myself that the companionship somehow made up for the lack of an adult male presence at home. It even occurs to me that Mother understood this and never really made an issue of my hanging out there.

The gas station, like the diner, really was like a lodge, with the succession of proprietors its masters. You couldn't be black-balled, but you could be frozen out. You had no trouble knowing if you weren't welcome, and if you were welcome you felt (I surely did) as if you had acquired real status in the world. It seems to me now that I said very little in those days. I was either a mascot or a pale Greek chorus of one, supplying laughs and exclamations as required and appropriate. But on those rare oc-casions when I said something sensible or offered a fact, of which I had a large supply, the proprietor or one of the visiting elders would say, "Hey, the kid's right." It was better than scoring one hundred on a test.

The literature of the place was a collection of anecdotes, told and retold—stories from the Hammondsport past, from the days around the station itself. After a while there was no way to tell how large the originating grain of truth had been, before the story-tellers got hold of it, but the stories were wonderful. Did one of the town drunks really take a swig of embalming fluid, imagining it to be something else, the night the funeral parlor burned down? Did Mrs. Bauder really drop her diamond ring down the outhouse and did all the complications ensue as re-cited? Were the goings-on in the livery stable after the band con-cert accurately reported? Was the Model A really assembled on the schoolhouse roof that Halloween? I don't know. I only hope so.

Then there were the catch-phrases and the code words that came into fashion and died of overuse but that for a brief time were like lodge rituals, cryptic but not hidden. They made almost no sense out of context; they didn't make much sense in context. But one day, for example, a Wallace Beery-like figure who owned a gravel truck drove into the station and caught sight of a really amateurish soapbox racer I had been trying to build out of an orange crate. "Suffering aye-holes," he said in a bellowing voice, "a pickin' box on wheels!" This driver was already a legend at the station because he liked to run a little bulk motor oil over a candy bar before he ate it, on the grounds that the oil soothed his stomach. "A pickin' box on wheels!" repeated in his own bellowing accents became an all-purpose cry, like "Aloha," around the station for weeks afterward. Then, like "Hubba hubba," another station favorite, it died of exhaustion.

I envied Barry Levinson being able to re-enact his diner years and I understand that one or two of his old gang came to see themselves played on the screen. I have often wished I could stage a reunion of the Atlantic filling station crowd, but it is impossible. Most of the proprietors I knew did not live to see gas at a dollar sixty a gallon. Wally and Bud are still around town but we couldn't make a quorum. Howie, another of the regulars, died of a heart attack much too young. The two Bills and Jim and Ray and the others of us are dispersed across the face of the country.

The last time I can remember any large number of us being together was on a grey, dank afternoon in 1941. Howie had managed to get hold of his family's durable Essex and seven of us piled in to go bowling up at Bath. When we got back to the station at the end of the day, we found everybody else leaning into the radio, straining for more details about the Japanese attack on Pearl Harbor. Not one of us knew for sure where Pearl Harbor was, but it changed the lives of all of us. I left Hammondsport a few months later and when I finally came back in 1946 the station looked like a different place. The grease rack had been enclosed and there wasn't a soul around I knew.

The Park Theater

It is no longer possible to tell where the Park Theater was. The business block it was in on the north side of Pulteney Park has been redesigned so that no trace of the theater remains, and in its space there is instead a dentist's office. Like the town band, the Park Theater did not long survive the Second World War and, like small-town theaters all over the country, it was principally a casualty of television. Schine's Babcock Theater in Bath is gone as well, and I'm told there is no longer a walk-in movie house between Elmira and Rochester, not even in Corning, where there used to be more than one. There are a few drive-ins but these, too, are feeling the pinch of the video cassette players. If you think, as I do, that there is no substitute for watching a movie in a theater, it is a glum state of affairs.

The Park never looked like a temple of magic. It was no wider than an ordinary retail store and like many of the pioneer movie houses I'm sure it began life as a store. It was owned by a man in Rochester who leased it to various local operators. The theater didn't even have its name in lights; there was only a meager wooden marquee (no movable letters) with "Park" painted on the front panel by Claude Jenkins, a barber at the Gent's Club who in his spare time did most of the business signs in town in the thirties and forties.

Temple or not, the first time I went back to Hammondsport

and saw that the marquee and the theater had disappeared without a trace I felt as if a part of me had disappeared as well. Larry McMurtry in his novel and Peter Bogdanovich in the film version of *The Last Picture Show* provided a very moving epitaph for the small-town movie theater and, although the one in the film was grander than the Park, the Texas town could have been Hammondsport, sounding the same last hurrah for a special time in American life.

My first-ever moviegoing experience was disastrous. I was, I think, five and my grandmother took me to see a dreadful documentary about Africa. The Park had no rest rooms of its own; you had to leave the theater and walk next door to the Hammondsport Hotel and use theirs. There was a long and, as it turned out, excruciating sequence in which a native in a loin cloth discovers wooden matches and lights them one after another, to watch them flare up. I can see the scene even now, vividly, and I can also remember how desperately I needed to be escorted to the rest room at the Hammondsport Hotel. I made it, but not a moment too soon and in some humiliation. Despite the circumstances of the evening, my love affair with the movies began right there and was nourished by another decade of heavy attendance at the Park. It was about as drably minimal as movie theaters ever get, but it might as well have been a temple of magic and the visions on the screen were gaudy, thrilling, and unforgettable.

There is much about television that is important, instructive, and engrossing, though I often regret that the medium seems to be homogenizing the country, blurring and blending all but the strongest regional accents and differences and making Johnny Carson's jokes as intelligible in Hannibal, Missouri, and Hammondsport as in Hollywood. These days Hammondsport even has its own cable system for better reception. But when I drive around the village square and remember the excitement that the Park Theater represented in my life, I tell myself that the later generations, brought up on the small screen and the VCR, will

104

never know how much they missed. Even the city youngsters with their access to the multiscreen cinema complexes in the shopping malls might find it hard to believe just how central to the life of Hammondsport "going to the show" was. (And it was going to the show, not to "the movies," "the theater," "the talkies," or "the films," and certainly not "the cinema.")

The Park stood on the north side of Pulteney Park, separated from Grimaldi's Restaurant on one side by a flight of stairs that led up to Jim Jones's barber shop and some apartments. On the other side was another store that housed various tenants over the years. Beyond the store was the three-story Hammondsport Hotel, which later burned, spectacularly. You could take a short cut through the hotel's tap room to the rest rooms if it was really urgent. Or you could go the long way around through the lobby if you had more time and you didn't mind missing a longer piece of the movie. I always hated having to walk through the bar under the amused glances of the customers who knew where you were going and why, but I also hated to miss more of a movie than I had to.

The Park had no more than one hundred fifty seats and they were hard, unpadded, and splintery. The projection booth was reached by a vertical, built-in ladder beside the one and only aisle, just past the tiny ticket booth. The projectionist of the time, a loping and Ichabodian figure named Franklin, was the first really indefatigable movie buff I ever met. At home he had a sixteen millimeter projector and a collection of silent newsreels. He gave showings, mostly of World War I troops marching in a jerky, wrong-speed way. I thought them a little monotonous without sound, but Franklin sat hypnotized. On the nights I attended the Park, Franklin used to let me open the hand-operated curtain. On the first fanfare of Fox Movietone News I pulled the rope and then swaggered up the aisle to my seat like someone who had done a very great work. It was my start in show business.

The bill changed three times a week. There was a double feature on Friday and Saturday, two westerns if the management could arrange it, and a serial. I can remember one glorious week-end when the bill was two Buck Jones features *and* a Buck Jones serial (*The Phantom Riders*, a phantom voice whispers to me over the decades). There was likely to be a comedy or a musical on Sunday, Monday, and Tuesday night and a melodrama on Wednesday and Thursday night.

The prints that finally made their way to Hammondsport were always near the end of their useful lives, worn and torn, and flecked with white where the tails of the prints had been allowed to flap by lazy projectionists. No print was without several splices and one or more of them invariably gave way in mid-screening. In the darkness we would hear Franklin bellowing with rage and tossing film cans around the booth. Years later I realized that the Park never played any MGM films, probably because of territorial booking arrangements that gave the MGM exclusively to the Babcock in Bath and the Elmwood at the other end of the lake in Penn Yan. The Babcock was much fancier than the Park. It was wide enough to have side aisles and the seats were plush. It made a dignified setting for those elegant white title cards that MGM used on even its lesser films. I saw the first several of the Andy Hardy films there, and later I understood just how well they epitomized Louis B. Mayer's view of the ideal family in the ideal community in the ideal society. I envied Andy, or Mickey Rooney, and I fell in love with all his girls. When I wrote a book about how the movies had changed under the impact of television, I subtitled it *Whatever Happened to Andy Hardy,* because the world the movies were picturing in the sixties and seventies bore no resemblance to Judge Hardy and his kindly domain in Carvel, Idaho, where there was never a problem that could not be happily resolved in the last reel.

Occasionally the Babcock dropped its dignity a little. I must have been thirteen or fourteen when a traveling sex education film complete with live lecturer played the Babcock, with separate performances for men and women—to avoid embarrassment to either sex, the ads said. I suspect now that the entrepreneur four-walled the house, as they say, renting the theater for a flat fee and keeping all the box office receipts. There was a nurse in residence (a woman in a nurse's uniform anyway)—in case the material was too graphic for the customers, the lecturer explained. Sure enough, a man apparently fainted during the talk. "Down here, quick!" the speaker barked authoritatively at the nurse. Even then, I would have bet a quarter that it was all a fake, but it was a delicious fake. The whole show was obviously a way to get some sex into the cinema in that heyday of the Hays Code with all its restrictions on content, especially sexual content.

I remember even now some of the lecturer's rapid-fire patter. "If you can't remember all this," he shouted, waving a booklet which cost extra, "tack it to the headboard and read it as you go along." He also remarked, to great laughter, "You never saw a tomcat running around with a jar of Vaseline," a reference I thought I understood, although I couldn't be quite sure.

The Park was still limping on when I left in 1942, but its audiences fell away and eventually it gave its own last picture show. It was briefly converted to a teen canteen, known colloquially as Myrt's and Gert's, I was told, and the premises were later absorbed into Shaw's Furniture Store. The Babcock struggled along for a few years longer. Then on one trip to Hammondsport I saw that the Babcock's marquee had been removed, which made that stretch of the street look like a plucked eyebrow. The theater was then trying to stay alive by offering soft-core skin flicks in midweek and family fare on weekends. But the schizophrenic menu did not help; television would not relax its glassy grip, and now there is no trace of the Babcock at all.

I'm sorry there haven't been more serious studies of the effects of the movies on all those of us who grew up in the days before television and who thus consumed a steady diet of motion pictures. I'm sure, for example, that many novelists write a good deal more visually in terms of scenes and confrontations, because they were influenced consciously or unconsciously by the movies they began to see in childhood.

But if the movies have been a way of seeing, as the critics say, they also—more in the thirties, forties and fifties than now—influenced the way we thought and felt about life and the world and the way things were. They set our romantic ideals for us and defined the good life (which looked quite a lot like California, wherever you lived). The umbrella of shared, agreed values that seemed so evident in the Hammondsport of my growing up was endorsed and taken for granted and therefore promulgated by the movies. The values didn't have to be spelled out in the dialogue (although they frequently were)—they were acted out.

The profound difference between American movies up through the early sixties and American movies since then is that they formerly spoke with one voice and now they speak in many voices: cynical, sentimental, fantastic, realistic, existential, traditional, arch-conservative, arch-liberal, patriotic, nihilistic. It is certainly healthier, with no single authoritarian voice predominating, but it can be confusing.

I well remember standing in church one Sunday morning in 1934 and, with the rest of the congregation in St. Gabriel's, reciting a solemn oath to obey the strictures of the Roman Catholic Legion of Decency against Condemned and Morally Objectionable films. (Secretly I thought it would be exciting if one ever came near Hammondsport but I was afraid it was not likely and I was right.)

In reaction to the Legion of Decency the Hollywood studios adopted that famous Hays Code by which they would make their films thereafter. It decreed, among other things, no nudity, no profanity, no glorifying of crime or criminals, no crimes or sins to go unpunished, either by the law or by poetic justice. The code was so specific it explicitly banned stories about farmers' daughters and traveling salesmen. In a more general way the code confirmed that we all lived in a God-centered world adhering to Judeo-Christian principles. The result was a steady repetition, implicit or explicit, of certain truths, such as that truth itself and justice were always served in the end. Crime didn't pay; adultery and other transgressions were punished one way or another; self-sacrifice was worth it; mothers were good, father knew best, and the good guys always won or never did worse than break even.

The business of the movies then as now was escape, diversion, reassurance, and uplift, and in its own way the code reinforced all those qualities. Whatever was happening in the real world, there were happy endings in the silver-lit darkness. Sure, a movie could require three or four hankies, an enduring measure, but it was usually a good cry because good people tended to die prettily and nobly.

Despite the restrictions the code placed on the creative freedom of the filmmakers, a lot of wonderful films came along in the thirties and we're still watching them: the Astaire-Rogers musicals, the works of W. C. Fields and Charlie Chaplin, the melodramas from Warner Brothers and the films of Frank Capra from Columbia. They were lovely then and they are lovely to see now, with their simplicities, naiveties, and their flaws (if any) frosted over with our fond memories.

If there was a downside, and I began to see later that there was, it was in part that the movies created a quite unreal idea of what the real world was like. The good guys don't always win, to take a minor example. Father may not know best and Mother may be an absolute horror. Good looks are not the most important thing in considering a romantic partner. But perhaps the most nefarious lesson that the movies taught, implicitly, and that the movies and television still teach, is that only violence solves problems. Violence became a kind of convention, a kind of action that was to some extent a substitute for more subtle dramatic material the movies couldn't handle. It was all understood to be make-believe, of course. Bang, bang, you're dead. But how make-believe was it? What seeped into our heads while we sat on those splintery seats in the Park Theater? It seemed to me that the real world, once I got out into it, required a certain amount of re-learning. Many of the confident assurances I'd had from the movies took some unlearning.

Yet I am carried back to the Park Theater very often these days. So many of the films we watched, the awful ones as well as the classics, keep recirculating on television, preventing the used car commercials from colliding head-on in the middle of the night as I've often said. One of the cable stations in Los Angeles has been running a lot of the stupendously corny musical shorts that were made in the early 1930s. I thought they were terrible when they were shown at the Park Theater—we had standards then, too. But now I watch them in wistful fascination. Once in a while, idly turning the television dial late at night, I come upon a scene (in glorious black and white) that not only takes me back to the Park but puts me in my favorite seat (way inside, at the left-hand wall, in about the eighth row back), and for a small moment I am that kid again, feeling what I felt then. It is eerie, but nice.

After all these years, the love that began at the Park is still with me, and even now there are few excitements to match for me that moment when the lights go down and the curtain opens. I regret that I'm not as young and trusting and innocent as I was when I first watched movies at the Park. But then again, the movies could use a little more innocence, too.

The Town Band

When I saw Meredith Willson's *The Music Man* on Broadway, I realized in a dazzling flash that some eastern equivalent of Professor Harold Hill must have come through Hammondsport in the mid-1930s. One day there was no band at Hammondsport High School and overnight, so it seemed, there was. The next day there we all were, learning to make sounds on instruments our families had been persuaded to buy in easy installments. Our teacher was a handsome and full-figured woman named Miss Marian Watkins, with whom I was so infatuated at age eleven that I would have taken up the glockenspiel, the tuba, the fife, or all three if she had asked me. I was already listening to jazz and big band music. Harry James and Louis Armstrong were idols of mine, so when Miss Watkins indicated that she eagerly required another trumpet player, it seemed a wonderful choice.

I acquired a brand-new but cheap horn that was at the bottom of some manufacturer's product line and that had a sour tone I now choose to believe was only partly of my making. As a premature perfectionist I practiced until family and friends must have been at their wits' end. I mastered "My Old Kentucky Home," my first blatty solo, in record time. Professor Hill's little group in River City made its debut with a shaky but identifiable and self-taught rendering of Rubinstein's "Melody in F." Our school band conquered a series of easy marches, with "Our Di-

111

rector" as our first hit. The title itself will mean little to the public at large, but the fanfare-like strains of that march may sound vaguely familiar because it has probably been played by every high school band in the country.

Our band acquired basic uniforms, white duck trousers and purple capes and visored hats (purple and white were the school colors). We marched in innumerable parades and played at school assemblies and basketball games.

Miss Watkins moved on to greater glories, breaking my heart or at least cracking it a little. The new music teacher was D. Elwood Martin, who was just out of Fredonia State Teachers College and who played both cornet and tuba. One Saturday morning he drove Mother and me to Syracuse, where I traded in that first cheap trumpet for a King Master Model II cornet, which cost $160, a lot of money in 1940, and which I still have.

I got a little better as I went along, but I should have listened to the early tip-off that the new Harry James was not on his way. The key word in any brass player's vocabulary is embouchure, that subsurface callus on your upper lip that lets you blow high, hard, and long. But no matter how long I practiced, my lip never developed any real staying power at all. I was good for about ten good minutes, and then it was pray for low notes. The lip came back, of course, like your wind after a hard run, but a couple of high C's later I was done for again. It may be that a different mouthpiece, different instruction, different exercises might have helped me. But who knew, then? I thought I just needed more hours of practice. Later in life I consoled myself that the discipline and the hard work had been good for me. The lessons in earnestness spilled over into other things I wanted to achieve and had to work hard at.

I have no doubt that that was true. But what all those hours practicing on the cornet also taught me was that there are some things in life you're going to be good at and some things you're not, no matter how hard you try. What you have to hope for is that there is pleasure somewhere in the trying. And the cornet did give me a lot of pleasure and relaxation for more than forty years, however wearying it may have been for the family as I tootled along with my Dixieland records. But there is even more to it than that: making music collectively, in a small amateur orchestra, in a marching band, in the living room with the family, is one of warmest satisfactions I've ever found in life. I cherish every moment of the music, even when I was sounding really terrible on "Mexicali Rose" in an orchestra that met for a while in the undercroft of the Presbyterian Church.

Once I had my grand new cornet, my dream was to play in the town band. The band had been giving concerts in the bandstand in Pulteney Park, the village square, on summer Saturday nights since the turn of the century. The cars would arrive an hour early to get parking spaces on the four sides of the square. Later the honking of horns became applause. On windless nights, the sounds of the music and the car horns would carry all over town. I can remember falling asleep hearing the faint high notes of the cornets and the clarinets. When I was very young, it was the week's thrill to be walked to the concert and provided with a bag of Grimaldi's popcorn.

Even in the late years of the Depression, those Saturday nights in Hammondsport were festive. The kids from the summer cottages came to town to check out the action, farm families came down from the hills to do the week's shopping. A few of the families still made the trip in horse and wagon, parking in the stables behind the Sheather Street stores. The town small fry ran around the bandstand, playing tag and screaming, or climbed up the railings to look over the musician's shoulders. One summer the word went around that if you sucked a lemon in front of the clarinetists they puckered up so they couldn't play. I always wanted to try it but the one time we brought a lemon we were chased away before we could make the experiment.

The players were older men. Several of them lived in Bath and had played in what was once a full-time band and orchestra stationed at the Soldiers' and Sailors' Home, which was built in

1878 and now is a major Veterans Administration facility. There were local men as well. Herb Emilson, whose family owned and operated the Hammondsport Hotel, played clarinet and was the manager of the band. His brother Norm, the station agent down at the Bath & Hammondsport Railroad depot, played saxophone. Irwin Young, who worked at Taylor Wine and was mayor of Hammondsport for a while, played the bass drum. Ned Hallenbach, whose elegant brother Bob gave ballroom dancing classes in the Hook and Ladder rooms opposite the bandstand, played upright alto. There was one woman—Doris Layton, who played the flute.

It would never have occurred to me to ask for an audition. I lacked anything like that kind of confidence, and the runs and the high notes that the cornetists achieved seemed permanently beyond my gifts. But Fate tapped me on the shoulder, as it will when you least expect it. Mr. Martin, the new music teacher, had been recruited to play tuba in the town band and, noting a shortage of cornetists, recommended me to Herb Emilson and the conductor, Dave Thomas. What he had detected (I think, looking back) was that I could sight-read like a whiz, even if I couldn't always execute what I could read. The band had only one rehearsal before a concert, and you had to be a quick study. Herb Emilson invited me to sit in. The band rehearsed on Friday nights in a room with a low tin ceiling on the second floor of the village jail, alongside the Glen creek. Even with all the windows open, the din was so terrible it's a wonder we weren't all left permanently hearing-impaired. The wages—or mine—were seventy-five cents for the rehearsal and a dollar and a quarter for the concert, to be paid in a lump sum at the end of the season.

Dave Thomas, the leader, was a perky, crusty, red-faced Welshman in his mid-70s. He had an artificial leg, one of the old-fashioned kind not hinged at the knee, so he walked with a swinging, piratical gait. He conducted with a stubby baton in one hand and his cornet in the other. He had no teeth; at least he didn't wear them when he played. But his lips were as leather

114

and he could play louder and longer than the rest of us combined. In his youth, Dave had travelled with a circus band and that's the hardest playing there is: the music has to be fast and continuous. I imagine the circus years gave Dave his tireless embouchure. Eventually he settled down with the Soldiers' Home band and orchestra and then retired, except for the Hammondsport concerts. It was from Dave that I took my cornet lessons on Saturday mornings, bicycling up to Bath and back so long as the weather was good, with my King Master Model II in the basket.

At my first rehearsal with the town band, on a stifling July night, there was a lot of good-natured kidding about what the band was coming to, taking in children. I sat beside Manley Bennett, a contemporary of Dave's who had been a printer until he lost his right arm to blood poisoning. He had had a special bracket attached to his trumpet so he could both hold it and work the valves with his left hand. He produced a marvelously sweet and liquid tone and like Dave he could play anything. He and Dave took the solo parts and I was the second cornet, supplying harmony and the occasional countermelody. We played music Dave had obviously been hoarding for years. Some of it, I imagine, he had rescued when the VA decided to abolish the resident band. I saw that the copyright and publication dates on the parts were often from the 1890s and the early years of this century. There were all the Sousa marches, naturally, and medleys of operatic tunes, Gilbert and Sullivan, Strauss waltzes. The individual parts, as Dave handed them around, were usually brown with age, and once in a while I would find that my part had been corrected in pencil, a ghostly assist from a horn player long gone. The only contemporary pieces Dave had acquired were "The Beer Barrel Polka" and "Oh! Johnny," but nobody seemed to mind.

It was a wonderful trial by fire for me, a forced-draft musical education, and I was unutterably and probably insufferably proud. The two dollars a week was the first *professional* money I had ever earned, as I thought of it, the first that did not involve raking leaves, washing cars, or peddling newspapers or the *Sat-*

urday Evening Post. Not only that, I got a uniform. The uniform I was issued, complete with Sam Browne belt, brass buttons, and garrison cap, was the smallest Herb Emilson had in stock, but it would still have fit someone twice my size. I was already almost six feet tall, but I only weighed about one hundred twenty-five pounds. I used to say I could hide by turning sideways. In the uniform I must have looked as if I were poking my head out of a blue pup tent. The blue was not colorfast, as I learned when we marched in a pouring rain one Fourth of July. When I came home my skin was blue from neck to ankles.

The high point of the band year was the Saturday of Labor Day weekend. It was not only the last concert of the season, it was also the day when the band always drove over to Montour Falls to play for the annual outing of the Shepherd Electric Hoist Company. It was a fish-fry, held in a glade just outside the village limits because the village, I think, was dry. Beer and other beverages were served in quantity from the trunks of automobiles. On my first outing I would have been even freer with the beer than I was, but Dave Thomas fixed me with a stern Welsh glare. I was fifteen but looked twelve. Despite his disapproval I drank enough to become extremely joyful. Dave knew from experience that when we got back to Hammondsport for the Saturday night concert after our exhausting afternoon in Montour Falls, the band members would simply not be up to "Victor Herbert Favorites" or "Orpheus in the Underworld," with their swift changes in key and tempo and their intricate instructions for repeats. Instead we played "The Beer Barrel Polka" over and over again, interspersed with marches we knew from memory. After the concert we adjourned to the back room of the tavern at the Hammondsport Hotel, where Herb Emilson gave us our pay for the season and offered drinks on the house. But I knew better than to push my luck and I headed home. By the time I got there the effects of the beer had worn off and my mother asked no difficult questions. I did feel very much like a musician, and it seemed to me that in that summer with the band, I had come of age in several ways.

I had had a terrific time. I had discovered the joys of beer and fish fries. I knew (or I think I knew) that I would never be as good a cornet player as I wanted to be; the lip wasn't there. But I knew there was marvelous pleasure to be had in the playing. And I had shown myself that there were rewards at the end of all those scales and arpeggios in *Arban's Celebrated Method for the Cornet*. I'd just about held my own in the company of adult musicians, and that was an exhilarating feeling. I was doubtless still a tall, thin kid to the men in the band, and nothing pejorative intended. But as I saw it I was no longer a boy from school.

After forty years of lip service to the cornet I decided it was time for a change and I started taking clarinet lessons. It is thrilling *not* to have trouble hitting the high notes. But I still take out the cornet now and again and blow a few notes in celebration of Dave and Manley and my other pals on the bandstand.

The town band did not survive the war. There are no longer regular Saturday night concerts in Pulteney Park. I suspect the end of the band concerts can be read as symptomatic of all kinds of changes in the society, most especially the dispersing effect of the automobile and the rise of television and now the video cassette. What I'm sorry about, on behalf of any local child just taking up a musical instrument, is that joining the town band no longer exists as a sort of test dream, a stepping-stone toward even larger dreams that can be made to come true.

Cradled in the Cradle of Aviation

One of the thrills of growing up in Hammondsport in the thirties—and there were several—was that the sky was full of flying machines. The village still calls itself "The Cradle of Aviation" because it was here that Glenn Hammond Curtiss built some of the earliest successful airplanes, fragile things that led to the first seaplanes and the JN4's, or Jennies, the principal American trainer plane of World War I. The Curtiss Museum of Local History sells T-shirts that ask, "Wilbur and Orville Who?" In the thirties, Harvey Mummert's small experimental racing planes snarled through the air like the bumblebees they somewhat resembled. There were experimental blimps and occasionally an autogiro, that early form of helicopter which had both a rotor and a fixed low wing. Light planes practiced leisurely loop-the-loops on summer afternoons, appearing to poise forever upside down.

Curtiss was a Hammondsport boy who opened a bicycle repair shop in a shed and soon had branches in a couple of nearby cities. He progressed to motorcycles and in 1907, at Ormond Beach, Florida, set a land speed record of one hundred thirty-seven miles an hour. It was his success in building lightweight engines for his motorcycles that led him to aviation. The Aero Club of America asked him to see what he could do about engines for lighter-than-air craft. In 1908, Curtiss's plane *June Bug* made the first pre-announced flight of more than a kilometer, an achievement which earned him the Scientific American trophy.

Curtiss and his fellow pilots were soon giving exhibitions at Dominguez Field in Los Angeles and in San Francisco. Like many an Easterner, Curtiss found the winters in Southern California an improvement on the chills of upstate New York. He could work all year, so in late 1910 he opened a winter aviation camp in San Diego to continue working on what he called the hydro-aeroplane. The Wright brothers had sold the Army an airplane. Curtiss was determined to sell planes to the Navy. On January 26, 1911, Curtiss successfully flew his first hydro-aeroplane off the waters of San Diego Bay, and the seaplane was born. "Mr. Curtiss made several flights several hundred feet high and all the whistles blew," said an eyewitness account.

By a nice coincidence, I was living in California when, on the seventy-third anniversary of the flight in 1984, a pilot named Jim Dalby flew a replica of the A-1—the first hydroplane Curtiss delivered to the Navy—off the same waters of San Diego Bay. Watching the flight on television I had a double sense of the past revisited. It looked like a slightly larger version of one of those new ultralight planes I had seen grazing the surface of Keuka Lake when I was there the previous summer. It also looked like one of Harry Benner's photographs come to life, especially the shot of the Langley airplane lifting off from the lake at Hammondsport in 1914 with Uncle "Gink" Doherty at the controls.

But the flight of the replica of the A-1 provided me with yet another link to the past. My cousin Tony Doherty, one of Gink's sons, who is president of the Curtiss Museum, knew the flight was to take place and he sent me a photocopy of a page from a document called "Aviation Log Curtiss Hydroaeroplane Navy No. A-1, 1 July 1911–16 October 1912."

It was the last page of the log, and the columns, filled in in ink in a careful, identical hand, record flights sixty-five through seventy-seven, noting for each the weather and wind, the pilot

119

Professor Samuel Pierpont Langley's aeroplane, restored by Glenn Hammond Curtiss, lifts off the water of Keuka Lake at Hammondsport on October 1, 1914, with W. E. (Gink) Doherty at the controls. *Courtesy Glenn H. Curtiss Museum of Local History*

and his weight, the passenger and his weight, the time of day and the duration of flight.

On September 4, 1912, the A-1 flew five times, piloted throughout by Lieutenant T. G. (Ted) Ellyson, the first pilot trained for the Navy by Curtiss. The passenger on the day's first flight was Augustus Post, secretary of the Aero Club of America, which encouraged and underwrote early aviation experiments. The passenger on another flight was Lieutenant J. H. Towers, the third pilot trained for the Navy by Curtiss. As Admiral Jack Towers, he commanded naval aviation in World War II.

The passenger on a third flight is identified merely as M. Champlain. Then as now the name gets misspelled a lot, but Tony confirmed that it was (Francis) Malburn Champlin, my father. He was then twenty years old and the log says he weighed one hundred forty-five pounds. He and Lieutenant Ellyson took off at 4:25 in the afternoon and flew for six minutes, reaching an altitude of one hundred fifty feet.

Watching the tape of the television newscast of the replica in flight, I had a good idea of what my father's adventure in 1912 must have looked like. But I can only try to imagine what it must have felt like to be a young man flying above the lake on a clear September afternoon, with the wind out of the northeast at eight miles per hour and the whole world before you.

What I had never known until fairly recently was that Glenn Curtiss was apparently the model for Tom Swift, the inventor-hero of a hugely popular series of books that was launched in 1910 and, by other hands and in other modes, still goes on. According to John T. Dizer, Jr., who summed up his findings in a lecture to the Friends of the Colgate University Library in 1984, the initial Tom Swift books were written by Howard Garis, who had been assigned to the task by Edward Stratemeyer. The Stratemeyer Syndicate was a fiction factory that turned out series titles (Nancy Drew, the Rover Boys, and so on) by the hundreds. So far as I know, it still does.

Garis was born in Binghamton and grew up in and around Syracuse and was thus well-placed to know about Curtiss, Hammondsport, and Lake Keuka. Tom Swift's fictional home town was Shopton, on Lake Carlopa, and Dizer reported that the resemblance to the real places are evident. There are other linkages. Curtiss won an international air meet at Rheims, France, in 1909. Tom Swift won a similar meet in 1910. And there is the further coincidence that *Tom Swift and His Motor Cycle* was one of the titles that Garis, writing as Victor Appleton, turned out in the first year of the series. That same year, writing fast to keep young readers interested, Garis also spun tales about Tom and his Motor Boat, his Airship, his Submarine Boat and his Electric Runabout.

The Tom Swift series was an instant hit, as Dizer reported, and it is easy to see why. There was already a kind of folklore celebrating the lives of the actual young inventors like James Watt, who wondered what could be done with the steam from a teakettle and came up with the steam engine. By the late nineteenth century and into the twentieth century the inventor—Thomas A. Edison was the very model of the breed—had come to seem a typically American figure. He was a key figure in the country's dynamism, optimism, ingenuity, drive, and success. Tom Swift's inventions, like Jules Verne's dreams, were taken to be prophecies, not fantasies, and so they have turned out to be. Via Garis, Swift invented the laser beam and the picture telephone. If Tom Swift was wholly or partly Curtiss, Curtiss was certainly Tom Swift.

Curtiss, who died at only fifty-two in 1930, had by then left aviation and was developing the cities of Miami Springs and Hialeah in Florida. His decision to move his factory from Hammondsport to Buffalo so he could enlarge his production capacity to meet the demands of World War I caused some bitterness in town among those who couldn't follow him to Buffalo. But he remains an admired presence in Hammondsport, and the museum has an engrossing assortment of his motorcycles, his airplanes and other memorabilia. Tourists come in considerable numbers to look at the granite boulder, inscribed simply "Curtiss," that marks his grave in Pleasant Valley Cemetery, just up the valley from the field where he made his first flights.

In 1986, to celebrate the seventy-fifth anniversary of the first flight of the A-1, Hammondsport put on its own observances, including the flight off Lake Keuka of another replica of the A-1, piloted by a daring seventy-nine-year-old named Dale Crites. There was also a jet fly-over, a concert by a Navy band, a commemorative stamp, and a visit by Astronaut Wally Schirra. Like the original, the replica of the A-1 was a flimsy, balky thing of wood, cloth, and wire. It had a wingspan of just over twenty-six feet and you steered it by twisting your shoulder harness. You also prayed for no updrafts; the A-1 was flighty in every sense.

122

The grave of Glenn Hammond Curtiss in Pleasant Valley
Cemetery south of Hammondsport draws early aviation en-
thusiasts from throughout the world. Curtiss died in 1930
at the age of only fifty-two.

It was not enough to be inventive. You had to have nerves of steel
as well.

Hammondsport's little gala took place over the same Fourth
of July weekend when international festivities were going on at
the Statue of Liberty. I couldn't make it to either but given a
choice I would have wanted to be in Hammondsport, lifting a
glass of champagne to the small-town tinkerer who helped to
change the world.

The Noon Siren

The siren on the old, one-engine firehouse next to Smellie's Drug Store used to blow every day at noon. If you stood right under it you felt it was going to leave you deaf and shake your teeth loose as well. In the summers when we were very young it was the subject of a dare. We would run downtown to watch Chris Fogarty unlock the box, check his turnip watch, and push the red button that set the siren going. Chris worked for the village; the Fire Department was volunteer then, as it still is, though it now occupies a large and elaborate new station the present volunteers have built over by the head of the lake.

We would stand there, hands over our ears, screaming "Yahoo" as loud as we could, for the odd pleasure of having our voices drowned out by the siren. The siren still blows at noon, but it's across the valley at the new fire house and I can't quite see the present generation of small fry dashing over there to hear it. They have the different pleasures television brings right to their living rooms, although they can't possibly be as exciting as yelling "Yahoo!" to a siren.

The siren evokes a variety of memories for me. It blew the night in 1932 when Franklin Roosevelt was elected; Hammondsport was and is Republican, but FDR favored the repeal of Prohibition and so did Hammondsport, fervently. The siren blew and blew and blew the night a large piece of the business section

124

burned down, and from my bedroom window I could see the glow of the flames against the sky.

The siren was a signal, but it was also a kind of community symbol. It blew on patriotic holidays and on every Armistice Day at eleven in the morning, honoring war service and patriotism and peace, and I associate the siren's clarion sound with those things, too.

Someone has said you can embrace the past so tightly that you can't grasp the present, let alone the future, and it is a danger I try to avoid. But there's a difference between examining the past and retreating into it. The past is an engrossing subject, I think, because it has a way of seeming to change, just as the present changes or our expectations for tomorrow change. The past changes as the eye that looks upon it grows older or wiser or possibly some of both.

It was only years later, for example, that I saw how nearly impossible it must have been to keep a small town jewelry store afloat during the worst years of the Depression, which was why Peter Kapral sold fireworks in season. Like the siren, Pete had a role in Hammondsport's patriotic observances. His may have been the only jewelry store in history that also carried Roman candles and was popular with small boys. Pete was a short, sallow man of Greek descent who lived in Bath but commuted to Hammondsport daily and came back again on Saturday nights, bringing his wife to the band concerts.

Pete's store was next to Payne's meat market on Sheather Street and no longer exists. It was the classic small town business establishment with a recessed door and display windows on each side of it. Come June and the windows would be full of fireworks. There were cherry bombs, those lethal balls that exploded on impact. The big guys, as we thought of them then, used to roar through town in their jalopies, throwing the cherry bombs and terrifying everybody, with good reason. There were also firecrackers the size of hot dogs, with enough blast power to lift a tin can several feet off the ground or detach a few fingers. I retain very little nostalgia for the cherry bombs or the giant crackers, but the skyrockets and roman candles arching over the lake on a summer evening were very beautiful, I thought, and they are a tradition that continues.

One of Pete's best fireworks customers was the embalmer from the local funeral parlor. He used to come in the store and lean over the display with a cigarette drooping from his lips. It drove Pete crazy. He would bolt forward from his workbench in the back of the store when the man came in, then check himself in mid-step and merely say something cheerful, just to make the man turn around—usually as a sparky ash seemed ready to drop from the cigarette.

Pete called me "his little fireworks salesman." Actually there were several of us, seven- and eight-year-olds, who hung around the store (mostly in fireworks time). We never handled sales, but we talked up the merchandise for all we were worth. Pete also had a small collection of antique arms and I have a snapshot of four of us (in identical one-piece bathing suits for some reason), displaying an ancient pistol, held by me, and a heavy musket, held by the other three. Photographs are a blessing; I remember nothing about the moment, the weight of the gun, or anything else. I presume Pete took the picture, but this is guesswork. (Even the fireworks did not sustain the store. Pete closed the shop and opened another over in Watkins Glen.)

There was always a Fourth of July parade, of course—usually a march from the park to the Presbyterian cemetery on Main Street, where there was a long prayer, a longer speech, another prayer, also long, and the firing of rifles by the American Legion, followed by a rush of birds from the elm trees. In later years I blew "Taps" after the volleys, sometimes playing strain for strain, like an echo, with Bill Longwell or Ed Sustakoski, trumpet-playing pals from the high school band. If there was a second ceremony at the Pleasant Valley cemetery, as there sometimes was, we got to stand through two patriotic orations.

Bombast was still in style and the Revolutionary War was

The author, age seven or thereabouts, and his pals Richard Lanphere, cousin Pete Doherty, and Jimmy Hart, display ancient firearms owned by Jeweler Peter Kapral, in front of his store in 1933.

made to seem only yesterday. The flags, snapping in the warm July afternoons, could be taken as the faint echoes of long-ago musketry.

Even in those prewar days, the world was moving in on us, and by the last of the Fourths of July I spent at that lovely lake village World War II had actually begun. The oratory, it seems to me, grew more fierce and confident than before. Yet even then, if patriotism was taken for granted, the matter of war was not so simple.

The first world war was not yet twenty years in the past when

I was a boy, and it seems to me that Armistice Day in Hammondsport meant a lot. The siren blew at 11:00 a.m. that day—the hour, we were taught, at which the First World War officially ended. The church bells rang too, tolling slowly, and there was a silence in the village, though the youngest of us might not have known exactly why. Every year Laura Bailey, the town librarian, arranged a special display in the window—books about the war, including the poems of Joyce Kilmer and Rupert Brooke. One year she displayed a poster, made, I expect, by a high school art student, which carried the lines

> In Flanders Field the poppies blow
> Between the crosses row on row. . . .

The two lines, framed by a design of poppies and rows of white crosses stretching to the horizon, made a strong impression on me, although it was a jumble of feelings, romantic, peaceful, lonely, sad, and scary. The veterans of World War One, in their uniforms if they could still wear them, dominated the parades. There were several surviving Spanish-American War veterans in town and, well into the thirties, Hammondsport still had one Civil War veteran. We called him Daddy Griegs. He was said to have been a drummer boy and, in his late nineties, he was again the size of a child. Nearly blind, Daddy Griegs shuffled across town every day from his house to the post office, saying "Hey-hey" to everyone who greeted him, and naturally everyone did.

He boasted that he voted for Abraham Lincoln, which was doubtful unless he falsified his age, but he always added that he had voted Democratic ever since, which may have been true.

I can't be sure exactly how I felt about war and death on those distant Armistice Days, before all the experiences of later life crowded out or colored and redrew the innocent child's-eye view. Yet, even discounting the adult overlay on what the boy saw and felt, it seems to me now that the eleven o'clock siren produced in Hammondsport a melancholy silence that was more than a ritual observance. Spanish villages do not have a monopoly on their awareness of the great punctuations of birth and death. The intimacy of small-town life anywhere makes them inescapable. It still surprises me when my friends, especially those who grew up in cities, tell me they have a horror of going to funerals and confronting the fact of death. Several have said they never went to a funeral until they were well into adult life and lost a parent or a very close friend. But in Hammondsport, as in most villages, the acquaintance with death begins early. I have a clear recollection of attending my grandfather Masson's funeral when I was four. It is a memory of a gray glove, because the funeral director or one of the pallbearers was holding me by the hand at the back of the church during the Mass.

Dick Torrance, one of my classmates, was killed in a motorboat fire the year we were in the third grade and several of us went to his funeral. Like the Armistice Day poster, the funeral produced a tumble of emotions in me—curiosity (the waxy shell in the open casket), fear and sadness again, and the first penetrating intimations of my own death. But, competing with the gloomy emotions, I felt an almost swaggering pride at taking part in an adult ceremony. Funerals were village events, and so were births and marriages and holidays, all of them marking our years.

As the thirties went on, Armistice Day was already touched with foreboding, and it was not only the grownups who felt it. You couldn't listen to Lowell Thomas's nightly broadcast (a town and family ritual) without knowing that things far away were getting out of hand again. There was trouble in a lot of places, Ethiopia, Spain and China and Europe, and hardly a newsreel played the Park Theater that did not show troops parading in one capital or another. I tried hard to wrap myself in ball scores, pulp magazines, and the awkward but engrossing business of being twelve, but the news was inescapable, like rain in a leaky pup tent. The further I got into adolescence, the likelier it seemed that I might one day get to march in my own parade. And so it proved, for me and a lot of us who grew up with the noon siren.

As it happens, I haven't marched in any parades or worn my uniform since I got out of the Army in 1946. By now the only items I could still wear would be the necktie and the shoes and socks and the Eisenhower jacket that was too big to begin with. Armistice Day is now Veterans Day, of course, and I find it hard to know what to think. I speculate about the lives that might have been for Reg Wood, my college roommate Jack Adikes and the other friends who died in the war. There are still the tyrants and the kings, as Steven Vincent Benet said in a poem. There is hardly a moment you can call peaceful anymore, taking the whole globe into consideration. Peace of mind appears to be a permanent casualty of our genius at devising mayhem. But there are other casualties, including the ability to sustain an innocent optimism much beyond the age of three.

Growing up in Hammondsport I was sure there were un- ambiguous distinctions between truth and falsehood, good and evil, and that the distinctions were valid for international rela- tions as well as private matters. The issues of war were clearer then, and peace was more than a nervous truce.

Things were never as simple as memory makes them, of course. But I think wistfully of the days when history could still be interpreted as a long march, often deflected but never ulti- mately disturbed, out of the primitive darkness toward a dream of peaceful, civilized perfection. Hammondsport, commencing with a handful of pioneers in a virgin valley, was part of that long march, and most things were as sharp and clear as a siren at high noon.

The Flood

It seemed to me in later years that the flood of July 1935 could have been the basis of a funny movie, despite the similarity in plot to Alexander MacKendrick's *Tight Little Island*. The flood has been the most newsworthy event in the modern history of Hammondsport. It was my introduction to natural drama on a large scale, a drama in which I played a minor supporting role—a sort of carry-on. It was the most exciting event of my young life, and I am stunned and subdued to realize that it took place more than a half-century ago.

As I learned from reading the newspaper accounts later, there had been a drought that year extending from late spring into early summer. On the weekend of July 6 and 7, 1935, the drought broke. All Saturday a drenching rain fell. The rain stopped for a while during the day Sunday, yielding to that sweltering heat that feels steamier in upstate New York than any other I've ever experienced. A new cloudburst hit Sunday night and it rained for six hours, with dazzling flashes of lightning and rolls of thunder that shook the walls.

Toward midnight, there was a pounding on our front door. It was Fred White, the part-time hired man who tended our furnace in the winter and did yard work and odd jobs in the rest of the year. He drank a little from time to time and had been known to come by the house at odd hours, asking for an advance on his pay. At first Mother shouted through the door and asked what he wanted. But it was obvious very quickly that he was sober and scared.

"It's a flood. You got to get out, ma'am," Fred said. Fred lived with his mother, Molocky White, in a crackerbox of a house that hung on the edge of the glen creek. The creek fell through a high and handsome gorge at the west edge of town, made a sharp left turn at the top of Church Street, a little way from Fred's house, and then flowed down past the business section to the lake. Normally it was no more of a trickle than you could leapfrog across easily, and the retaining walls were made of piled stones, like a country fence.

But the heavy and ceaseless rain and the runoff from the hills above the glen had turned the creek into a torrent and torn out the bank where the creek made its turn. The water had already taken away Fred's house and he had got his mother to safety just in time. Our house was at the foot of Church Street, which sloped downhill from the creek, and the water was already running through our yard and rising.

Just after Fred woke us up and we were pulling on some clothes, my older cousin, Tony Doherty, came to the house in the eerie, rain-soaked darkness, and carried first my brother and then me piggyback to the house next door, which stood on higher ground. By then the water was creeping onto our front porch, and urgent adult voices were shouting against the noise that the house looked like a goner. But within minutes a good-sized tree, borne down Church Street by the rushing water, wedged itself across two maples in front of the house. The rocks and the silt quickly built up behind it and the accidental dam began to divert the water onto Orchard Street which ran alongside our house and was dirt-surfaced.

By morning the flood water had gouged Orchard Street more than seven feet deep. It looked like a new river bed. There were from one to ten feet of rocks, mud, and assorted debris covering most of Hammondsport. Our cellar was filled nearly to the rafters with an oozy muck that smelled worse, day by day, as it

The 1935 flood left five hundred barrels of brandy all over Hammondsport—one of them conveniently in front of my house (at left) at 51 Lake Street. The trees helped divert the flood waters away from the house. *Courtesy Glenn H. Curtiss Museum of Local History*

dried. But the house was intact and there was no water damage above the cellar. The dawn's most exciting revelation, however, was what the flood had deposited around town beside the rocks and mud. There were the barrels, the hundreds of barrels.

Up in the glen, just this side of a high waterfall, the Georges Roulet Winery, closed since Prohibition, had had a warehouse, still crammed with barrels of aging brandy. There were also some barrels of pomace, the seedy leavings of the grape-pressings, and these complicated the local life for the next several weeks. The flood waters had ripped through the warehouse and carried the barrels all over Hammondsport. We had eight barrels in our yard, and one of them, as the neighbors told us kiddingly, looked as if we had been trying to push it out of sight under our side porch.

The brandy was untaxed and therefore illicit, and the state troopers came in to try to protect the barrels, although they had plenty of other matters to attend to, including escorting Governor Herbert Lehman, who came through town to inspect the damage. The scenario for the next few days was of local men wandering around the debris carrying a brace and bit, some rubber tubing, and two or three gallon jugs. The barrels were monstrously heavy and it was easier and more surreptitious to tap them where the flood had left them. There were stories, possibly apocryphal, like the one about the two men from Penn Yan who, hearing about the brandy, had driven a motorboat the twenty-two-mile length of the lake, located a barrel and, with magnificent effort, rolled it through town and aboard their boat and transported it the twenty-two miles back to Penn Yan—only there to discover that they had commandeered a barrel of pomace.

As matters returned to relative normal, the local chief of police had more time to attend to the matter of the barrels. The business of locating and then camouflaging a brandy barrel for later tapping thus became a sport and a new art form. There were daily tales of games of hide-and-seek and hot pursuits across the rubble.

For a nine-year-old the brandy-chasing was only one of the flood's excitements. There were bulldozers, steam shovels, and dump trucks everywhere, trying to clear away the debris. There were chasms where the streets had been and rock piles where lawns had been, cars buried in mud. The whole lake had gone from blue to brown with the run-off. We picked our way around town, like explorers. Nine years later I was poking through rubbled towns in Germany that looked much the same. The flood caused several deaths elsewhere in Steuben County and in the region, but there were miraculously none at Hammondsport, although the property damage was severe. The local Bath & Hammondsport Railroad was knocked out for a year or so; bridges

Some of the brandy barrels and a good deal of debris from the July, 1935, flood ended up in front of the local movie house, the Park Theater, and Grimaldi's Restaurant, next door. *Courtesy Glenn H. Curtiss Museum of Local History*

and houses were destroyed, and it required the rest of the summer and beyond to bulldoze the village free of the outwash. The creek got a new high-rise concrete flood channel and it has behaved ever since.

But the vision, or the memory, of streets and yards strewn with barrels of vintage brandy (the official count was five hundred barrels, for a population of twelve hundred people) was, naturally, the stuff of enduring legend. Then, or subsequently, I developed the impression that the brandy was seen as a sort of cosmic consolation prize for all the havoc and dislocation. It was Nature's way of apologizing for letting things get out of hand.

When Hammondsport celebrated the fiftieth anniversary of the flood back in 1985, it was the brandy that continued to dominate the memories and the news stories. There is still, in fact, a vial or two of the flood brandy stashed away in Hammondsport cupboards. It was said at the time to be very good and potent, despite the rough voyage. It travelled well. Not long ago Cousin Tony, who had carried me to safety the night of the flood, presented me with a small, hand-labeled bottle of flood brandy, the size of the nips they serve on airliners. It is the last he had, he said. I intend to save it for some later anniversary of the flood or of the author, and I hope the consumed and the consumer will both have improved with age.

The B&H

Rummaging through a desk drawer, I came upon my permanent pass on the Bath & Hammondsport Railroad. It was a joke item, carrying on one side the line's alleged slogan: "Not as long as the others, but just as wide." I doubt that the slogan was original even when it was printed, but it still makes me laugh. The pass also bore a warning: "Not good for passage if the bearer is sober," which confirms my impression that the passes were issued for the hooting ride down from Bath and the noisy party that celebrated the re-opening of the B&H after the line had been devastated by the famous flood of July, 1935.

The B&H had begun life in 1872, when Captain Allen Wood and other local entrepreneurs sold one hundred thousand dollars worth of bonds to finance it. Wood was also a principal owner of the Crooked Lake Navigation Company, which ran steamers on the lake. The idea was that the B&H would not only carry wine and table grapes up to the main Erie line at Bath, it would bring day-trippers down to Hammondsport for a cruise up the lake to Penn Yan and back—the outings Hal Roach still remembers from his boyhood in Elmira.

The line was originally narrow-gauge. According to a history of the B&H, written in 1947 by the late Carol Wood, the wife of my scoutmaster, Harold Wood, from Troop 18 at Hammondsport, the freight had to be hand-transferred at Bath from the narrow-gauge B&H cars to the standard-gauge Erie cars. Then a clever hydraulic lift system was devised in which the cars could be lifted back and forth from narrow to wide-gauge wheels. It was still unsatisfactory and the B&H was rebuilt as a standard-gauge line in 1890. In 1908 the local owners sold it to the Erie Railroad which, as Mrs. Wood reported, wanted to cash in on the day-trip excursions. For a few years tourists arrived by the hundreds not only to take the steamers, but also to watch Glenn Curtiss test his early fragile airplanes.

But Prohibition, which was hard on Hammondsport in every way, was bad news to the B&H, as well. Wine shipments dropped to nil, of course. The passenger service was discontinued, a casualty of the rising popularity of the automobile and of the fact that visits to the wineries, another tourist attraction, were no longer possible. The last of the lake steamers burned at its dock in 1920, a casualty not only of fire and the rise of the automobile but also of the prevalence of the truck and the motorboat. Scuba divers still poke around the ruins of the steamer in the deep water at the lakefront.

In 1924, Dick Aber as station agent and Leon Jaycox as general manager took over the line under an agreement with the Erie and kept it alive—just—until things began to pick up in the wineries with the repeal of Prohibition in 1933. Only two years later the great flood hit, wiping out hundreds of feet of B&H track and several bridges. The line looked as good as dead. But there was a real as well as a sentimental need to keep the B&H alive. A quintet of local businessmen bought what was left of the B&H from the Erie, restored the trackage and bought a splendid locomotive, the 860. Uncle Charlie Champlin, my namesake, who was then president of the Pleasant Valley Wine Company, was one of the five new owners and, as a ten-year-old when these events were transpiring, I thought it was a blissfully fine thing for him to have done. I still do, as a matter of fact. Joined with him were Deyo W. Putnam of Putnam's Winery, Fred C. Taylor

138

of Taylor's, Robert H. Howell, a coal and lumber dealer, and Ulysses S. Arland, who became the general manager.

When, by late July of 1936, the bridges were rebuilt and new track laid, dignitaries and train lovers from all over the country were invited to the reopening bash. The B&H was waiting on its line at Bath as the dignitaries arrived. Lucius Beebe, a columnist for the *New York Herald Tribune,* a man of impeccable sartorial elegance and one of the great train lovers of our time (with a special appreciation of "private varnish," as private cars were called), was pointed out to me. He wore a fawn cutaway and a matching topper and boarded one of the bunting-draped flatcars as you might a royal carriage, en route to a coronation or a princely nuptial. With the band playing, the train set off, even more slowly than usual, on the eight-mile downhill run to Hammondsport, past the Steuben County jail and the poor house, with the whistle blowing, soot and cinders flying, champagne flowing, the band blasting away.

The whole population of Hammondsport and then some was waiting at the little Victorian depot and freight house at the lakefront. There were speeches, surely, but I'm pleased to say I don't remember a word that was said, or by whom.

Throughout the rest of my Hammondsport years the B&H was part of the rhythm of the town's life, and its tooting (two longs, a short and a long) for the Main Street crossing as it headed uphill to Bath around midday and again when it came back in late afternoon was something to set your hungers by, if not your clocks.

Engine 860, Mrs. Wood reported, proved to be much too heavy for the trackbed. Like ships, railroad engines are female, and she—rather than it—jumped the track frequently, even after a speed limit of ten miles per hour was set. Once she rolled over completely and the cost of righting her was something like one thousand seven hundred dollars, which actually sounds like a bargain but was a lot of money in the late 1930s. Number 860 was fuel-inefficient as well and eventually gave way to diesel switchers, a rise in efficiency and a grave decrease in glamor.

The reborn B&H carried no passengers, but visitors were sometimes invited to make the trip in the caboose. The speed limit was still no better than ten miles per hour and the round-trip made for a long day, especially if there was a lot of freight to be loaded and unloaded at Bath. Thanks to Uncle Charlie, I rode the caboose a couple of times. It was a mild thrill to stand on the rear platform and watch Hammondsport recede. It was a keener thrill to stand on the bottom step and hang on with one hand. But those were limited thrills to space out a slow afternoon and there wasn't much you could do to be helpful. It was mostly a matter of keeping out of the way and trying to ask sensible questions instead of silly ones. At Bath a couple of through trains would roar past on the Erie or the parallel DL&W tracks. Their length and speed and sound humbled the poky old B&H, but waving from the caboose at the passing trainmen made me feel big for a minute or two.

I was a little too impatient for the B&H in those days, a short-sightedness on my part. It was my brother Joe who developed a long, close, and passionate relationship with the B&H. Jo-jo, as he was known around town almost from the time he could walk, wasn't yet ten when he started riding the B&H every Saturday—rain, snow, or shine. He acquired a trainman's cap and overalls and a fullsized black lunch bucket. He left the house before eight and walked down Lake Street to the station. He helped load the small freight into the caboose if he could and was sometimes allowed to ride on the engine if there was switching to be done. Up at Bath, as the months went by, Joe got to know some of the Erie trainmen who had paused to drop or pick up cars. One of them invited Joe to ride an Erie freight up to East Avon, New York, spend the night with him and his wife, and take a morning freight back down to Bath. It was an adventure and the beginning of a long friendship. Years later when Joe was ordained a priest, the Erie conductor, Jimmy Moran, and his wife drove over to Syracuse for the ceremony and were honored guests at the luncheon afterward.

Even more years later, when I was back in Hammondsport one summer, I stopped at the B&H station to say hello to Norm Emilson, who was then the station agent and with whom I had played in the town band. Norm opened the office safe and took out a small black notebook. In it, in a small, meticulous hand, Joe had noted the numbers of all the boxcars the B&H had hauled on those innumerable Saturdays (and, in summer, other days) he rode the caboose.

During a couple of his high school summers, after we had moved from Hammondsport to the village of Cleveland on the north shore of Oneida Lake, Joe—still in love with railroads—took a job on a track gang of the O&W Railroad (the New York, Oswego and Western), mostly cutting brush and laying ties. He spent those months wearing a maddening patina of poison oak and poison ivy. Some of the senior residents of Hammondsport may still tend to think of Jo-jo as the apprentice engineer with the oversized lunch bucket rather than as Monsignor Champlin of the Chancery office. I have no doubt he feels the pull of those days as I do when things were tidy, or so it seemed, and the world ran on rails.

Even though I was never as attached to the railroad as Joe was, I dream about the B&H all the time. One of my psychologist friends found this fascinating, rife with meaning and possibly alarming. He may be right. It only seems to me that I am reaching back in sleep to something simple and exciting. Sometimes the B&H is unbelievably prosperous, highballing down from Bath with a hundred cars and achieving unparalleled speeds. (Forget that ten miles per hour limit.) Quite often the business is so great that there is more than one track and more than one train. Once in a while I dream that the B&H has gone off the tracks again rather spectacularly, although never with injuries or loss of life. This is interesting mainly because I never saw the B&H when it had actually been derailed. The dream ef-

141

fect is mostly comical. Now and then I dream that the B&H has left the tracks but hasn't been derailed; it's just wandering around town where there aren't any tracks, like a toy train that doesn't need any tracks. My psychologist friend, who spends his life wrenching out the deep meanings of dreams, professed to be baffled by this one. Trains off their tracks are supposed to suggest disorder, chaos, disorientation, and panic he once said, eying me quizzically. But another friend, Marilee Zdenek, who writes about the right brain/left brain division of our cerebral functionings and who encourages elaborate mental images as a way of coping with problems and of stimulating creativity, frequently uses the train (tracked or untracked) as a vehicle for imaginative voyages to new terrains of thought and feeling, and she thinks my imaginative and imaginary travels with the B&H are probably wonderful for me.

I don't often ride trains any more; not many people do. But I did take a train down to San Diego not long ago to do an interview, and the special pleasures of it rushed back upon me. It was not a very glamorous outing, yet I felt a strange, ancient excitement as I walked through the marble dignity of Union Station in Los Angeles. I associate train terminals with painful wartime goodbyes. This morning was the more pleasant because I would be back home that afternoon. From the train window the landscapes and seascapes I thought I knew looked quite different and newly interesting. It was also a novelty to have time to read, rather than nervously watching the speedometer and the rearview mirror.

As we rumbled down the coast I thought inevitably about the B&H, which was said to be known in slang as the Bums and Hoboes. It was a source of daily drama and potential danger in our lives. (All those warnings about keeping off the tracks—and the awesome discovery that a penny left on a rail would be flattened to the width of a quarter!) My psychologist friend who doesn't know quite what to make of my B&H dreams never lived in a small town and certainly never in Hammondsport, not on

142

that special day in late July, 1936. He missed the opportunity to run alongside the flatcars with the bunting on them, to hear the whistle blowing and the band playing, and to understand that on that extraordinary day the B&H was a carrier of magic.

As No. 860, polished as much as she could be polished, pulled up to the depot, I'd have said the B&H could do anything it wanted to do, go anyplace it chose to go. It was distinctly not just an overaged steam engine reduced to working in the minors after possibly more exciting experiences elsewhere. It was an object of power and majesty. Up at Bath it connected Hammondsport with the whole country.

I'm afraid the B&H has seen better days. The depot, the subject of many a postcard and tourist snapshot, is still standing and it is still the office of the B&H, but by now it also houses a dentist's office. The lakefront has been beautified and so many boaters and picnickers use the area that, for the safety of pedestrians, the train itself no longer comes all the way to the depot. The caboose, with "The Champagne Route" painted on it in elegant script, sits unused on a siding behind the depot and, the last time I saw it, it badly needed repainting. But, despite trucks and planes and cars by the tens of millions, the B&H continues to run and to give the village an iron link to elsewhere. It appears to be a born survivor, which may in some mystical way be what my dreams are trying to tell me.

Hard Times

Growing up in the Great Depression was not like growing up in any other time, and those of us who were there have been marked by it forever. In Los Angeles I have lived through two big earthquakes and I will never feel the same again about the good old solid earth. The earth is not solid and it is not to be trusted for a minute. The Great Depression was an economic earthquake and none of its survivors will ever be able to regard their economic security as rock solid. Arm yourself with life insurance, annuities, savings accounts, stocks, bonds, IRAs, Keoghs, CDs, and gold coins hidden beneath the mattress and you still know in your heart of hearts that there can be temblors in the earth and that the economy can leave you standing there in your BVDs. These thoughts introduce a certain tense humility to your life.

Before the Great Depression Hammondsport was as settled and stable as villages ever get to be: a place where people remained—where they were born and lived and died. But when I think of the Depression thirties I think of the transients, all those who made brief but sometimes indelible appearances in our lives, because of hard times.

There were of course the real transients, the vagrants, the knights of the road, unshaven and dirty from sleeping rough, asking at the back door for a bite to eat and volunteering to do any odd job as a way of paying. They sometimes frightened my mother, a woman living with two small children in a manless house, because their hunger and their unshaved faces made them look intense and threatening. But she always fed them. She never asked them to rake leaves or split wood; she was simply relieved when they moved on. I was relieved too, not because I was frightened (a little of that, maybe) but because they were frightening proof that a nice, comfortable world could fall apart. I used to think I was precociously insecure the way other children were precociously clever. Even before I was a teenager I collected worries like merit badges, and it was myself I saw asking for handouts. The image of the gray men sitting on the back porch stays with me forever, and the homeless I see on the streets now in the eighties are a visitation from my past.

One memorable spring another breed of transients, a caravan of Gypsies in brightly painted horse-drawn wagons, the men, women, and children dark and vividly costumed, made its slow way through Hammondsport. For me it could have been a lost circus hitting town by mistake, but the myths about Gypsies had preceded them and something like a panic took place. The telephone rang over and over again as neighbors called Mother to warn her about the danger. All the children in town, so it seemed, were pulled in off the street and all the doors were locked. I watched the caravan through the living room window. The legends were that the Gypsies would steal anything that was not nailed down or too heavy to lift, and that they kidnapped local children to make Gypsy slaves of them. It was high drama, partly because they looked so darkly dramatic, and with their wagons they seemed to have come from another world as indeed they had.

The Gypsies were tinkers and one of the men shouted that they would patch pots and pans and sharpen knives and scissors. You would have said they were offering the plague. But a woman up the street, who was thought to be crazy anyway, came out with a pair of scissors for the man to sharpen. As he worked, she looked around with a triumphant smirk, as if to say, "Sissies!" A few other neighbors ventured out with pots to be fixed, and it was if a spell had been broken. The caravan finally moved off, and nothing was stolen and no children were reported missing.

The Depression put all kinds of people on the road to Hammondsport and through it. A pair of wandering musicians, playing an accordion and a guitar I think, came through town every year for a little while. They went from street to street, playing and singing until they had a crowd and then passing the hat. Once a man who billed himself as a human fly passed leaflets around town and at an appointed hour, with a huge crowd gathered, climbed the facade of the Union Block. The building was only three stories high, but the climb looked dangerous all the same, as it was, and the suspense seemed to last forever. I thought then, and think now, it was a tough way to make a living.

But the transients I think about most were the families who came to town in the hope of work and who stayed awhile and then went on, in pursuit of some better hope and perhaps in flight from unpayable rent. They took the cheapest accommodations Hammondsport had to offer—mean, dark apartments above the stores in the business section; rickety houses or parts of houses on the edges of town near the marshy inlet or up the dirt roads leading into the hills.

Most of the families had school-age children and there was something exotic and exciting about them. A lot of them had come from the cities, as far away as the Bronx and Brooklyn and Newark, and they had tough, funny accents. At first they were aloof, uncertain how to get acquainted with kids who had been together since kindergarten. Or they came on strong, the boys did, playing up the hard, dangerous life in the cities as a way of showing us small townies that we didn't intimidate or impress them.

But it isn't in the nature of the young to sustain poses for long, and quickly enough Freddie and Albert and Bobby and Willis and a James or two and a Lillian, a Lorraine and a Patsy and the others became part of us. We usually didn't get to know their parents. They were hesitant figures in doorways or at the top of

146

the apartment stairs. Often the fathers were not to be seen at all. They had stashed their families in Hammondsport and were out foraging far and wide for jobs.

When I remember the kids who became particular friends, it's hard to sort out what I knew then from what I surmise now. I suspect now that Freddie Lang, who became a good friend, put on a kind of non-stop performance for us, acting out a charade of indifference to the world as it was. Freddie was a big, soft boy who looked like he'd got his growth before he was quite ready for it and it hadn't firmed. But he went around with an easy nonchalance that nothing seemed to shake. He was laid back decades before the term was invented. But the pose that everything was swell (or if it wasn't, who cared?) really was a pose. A lot of the time he came to school looking angry and exhausted, if you caught sight of him unawares. I would see him staring into space, and today I might guess that he was pursuing some relieving fantasy of real ease and permanence.

Freddie and his family and the other families who paused in Hammondsport in the 1930s had been forced to become urban nomads, sentenced to wander endlessly in search of an oasis in the economic desert. The rent man and the bill collectors were their most frequent visitors. Freddie once shouted through the door, "My folks aren't here," before he knew that I was the one who had knocked. Then he stepped into the hall quickly and closed the door behind him, so I wouldn't guess that his mother was there, although I was pretty sure she was. Freddie had obviously become part of the family avoidance system for stalling the creditors. He learned early to see the world without illusions. And then—literally overnight it must have been—Freddie and his family were gone. He hadn't said goodbye and he never wrote me from wherever they went next. I have an idea they left no forwarding address and didn't want it known to me or anyone else. We were both twelve, crowding thirteen, when Freddie moved away, and I thought of him taking his nonchalance to yet another school, attracting another crowd of temporary friends, eventually having to deflect yet another town's-worth of creditors.

Even in the best of circumstances, life is a set of unfinished conversations and interrupted stories. I've always wanted to know what Freddie's later life was like (and Albert and Bobby's and Lillian's). The optimist in me wants to believe that in time the nomads found their oases and settled in to stay. Historically speaking, it's not an unreasonable hope. Whatever else was true of World War II, it ended the Depression, creating jobs in and out of uniform. Hammondsport had already begun to pick up, even before the war began, as the wineries got back into business after Prohibition. I want to think that Freddie, made tougher and more self-reliant by those hard years, did just fine.

Not all the new arrivals in Hammondsport were sent to us by the Depression itself and the thin hope of jobs. There were those who came to take executive jobs at the wineries or at Mercury Aircraft, for example. Men like the great French champagne-maker Charles Fournier gave the town a wonderful cosmopolitan touch. Another friend, Harry Botsford, who became the sales manager at Pleasant Valley Wine, arrived with his hoarse-voiced metropolitan accents like an upscale refugee from Damon Runyon. Ralph Lefaiver, a retired Air Force officer who became liaison between the military and Mercury, could in his upright bearing and moustachioed elegance have been played by David Niven.

What is harder to explain is what winds of change blew Doc Meagher and his wife Estrella and their boy Little Sammy to town. Doc was a chiropractor and from all accounts a very good one, although my impression is that in those days the locals went to chiropractors furtively, so as not to get on the wrong side of the MDs, who then still made house calls. Doc was a cadaverous man with a deep, cadaverous voice. He smoked cigars and quarrelled extensively with Estrella, as the neighbors several houses away could not help hearing. She was short, plump, dark-haired but fair-skinned and (I speculate now) was surely of Spanish descent, although by the time she hit Hammondsport she retained the Latin temperament but no accent. She lived life at the top of her lungs.

Sam was exactly my age (five or six when the family arrived in town), and since the Meaghers lived only a couple of doors away he and I became best friends, usually united in mischief. It was Sam who announced that green tea could be smoked like tobacco, so we climbed under his back porch and got sick proving that this was not true. We were briefly fascinated by our bodily functions and watched each other perform them with solemn interest. Sam and I also once broke into a house (it is one of my darkest childhood memories). The house belonged to a nice elderly couple who were friends of my family and were vacationing in Florida. The details are vague but I think Sam just put a rock through the glass front door. It was mid-afternoon (we weren't allowed out after dark) and our forced entry was widely observed. Once we got inside we didn't really know what to do since adventure, not theft, was our game. We hadn't been there long when my mother and Estrella appeared, screaming, gathered us up and switched us with lilac branches all the way home.

At first I didn't understand Estrella's mood swings at all. She was either girlishly gay or deeply unhappy. But gradually, even at a tender age, I came to realize that she drank more than was good for her and it changed her. More than once she stood on her front porch and yelled for me to come see her. The first time I went in the house she said that Sam no longer loved her. "I want you to have all his toys," she told me, sobbing. "He doesn't like them any more." I couldn't believe my good luck. The Doc and Estrella, out of whatever complicated guilts they had about Sam, treated him extravagantly. They bought him a vast train set that was never wired up correctly, a movie projector that jammed before the first reel had gone through, a truck you could ride on, tin soldiers, a bike he couldn't ride yet. It was a dream. That first time, eyes glittering with greed, I picked up everything I could carry and staggered home before Estrella could change her mind.

I never had a chance to unload my haul. "Back!" my mother said. "They're Sam's, not yours—and Estrella will be sorry she gave them to you when she feels better." I took them back, hating every step. Estrella tried to make me keep them, but I could tell my mother had been right; Estrella was relieved to have Sam's toys returned. Sam wasn't around; I think the Doc had taken him out of the house to avoid Estrella's tantrum. When she called me over a couple of times after that, I rejected the toys but, like a pint-sized psychologist, tried to comfort her saying that I knew Sam really loved her no matter what she thought. Estrella yielded fresh tears at that idea and wandered off toward the kitchen.

To me, the Meaghers are like a picture puzzle with more than half the pieces missing. I don't know where they had come from (I'm not sure anybody knew), and I can't imagine how so unlikely a couple had ever met and married. Sam, an impish, blond-haired boy who looked like a refugee from "Our Gang," seemed to belong genetically to neither of his parents and perhaps he didn't. Years later, when I was reminiscing about the Meaghers with Hammondsport friends, someone said as if it were beyond question that Doc was a dope addict. If that was true, Doc was the first addict I ever knew and I didn't know it. Estrella, I suppose, was the first female alcoholic I ever knew, but I didn't know that at the time, either.

Then, like Freddie and his family, Doc just vanished. Estrella stayed on and worked in the tiny box office of the Park Theater. It was a brief, wonderful interlude for several of us because she always let Sam's friends in free. By then Sam himself had been taken to live with friends in another city, since it was obvious that he was not enjoying a traditional home environment. Estrella rented a small house down near the lake. It was next door to the chief of police, Billy Leary, which may have been a source of discomfort to them both. Eventually Estrella left town and I don't know what became of her or of Sam. The word drifted back that he had become a lawyer, although when I tried to locate him in the city where he was said to practice I could find no trace of him. It would make good sense if he has resettled in some new place where he has no past and no one will confront him with tales of the Doc or Estrella, or the housebreaking caper he pulled with what's-his-name from down the street.

Teachers

My own children were born in four states and two countries and they know Hammondsport only as amused visitors to the neat town where their father grew up, their mother spent her summers, and their parents met. Their own continuity has not been a place but a family, which was the one constant at a whole series of addresses before we finally came to rest in Los Angeles.

Yet one of the things that most characterized Hammondsport before all the social upheavals during and after World War II was its feeling of continuity. The past was not somewhere else. It had persisted into the present so that there was a kind of commingling of yesterday and today on those elm-lined and maple-shaded streets. You could hardly escape a strong awareness of generations succeeding each other and building on the patient labors of the past. By the thirties there were families who had sent two and three generations of workers to the wineries. If I had not been seized by an obsessive desire to be a writer, I would have represented the fourth generation of my family on both sides to go into the Pleasant Valley Wine Company.

But probably the best measure of the stability of life in Hammondsport is the fact that my mother and I, more than thirty years apart, had the same teachers for first, second, third, and fifth grades. The Misses Nina Arland, Harriet Zimmer, Marian (May) Hamilton and Mary van Etten must have been just beginning their careers when Mother was their pupil in the years be-fore World War I. They were getting on toward retirement when I became their student in the years before World War II.

I can sympathize with students who are chided in class for not being as neat, well-behaved, earnest, or quick as their older brothers or sisters. It was my mother I had to live up to, and it was a psychological weapon Miss Arland et al. used sparingly but with devastating timeliness. After a while they didn't even have to cite her by name; they could say "Charles!" with such a descending, discouraged inflection that the rest of the message could be left unsaid.

The four teachers were all local women who went off to nor-mal schools, as the teacher training colleges were called, and who came home to teach, and teach, and teach, and then, in retire-ment, to teach Sunday school or, in the case of Miss Arland, to become the town librarian. Miss van Etten lived to be one hundred and died in Florida only a few years ago.

Miss Arland was the very model of the spinster schoolmarm, with horn-rimmed glasses and brown hair pulled into a bun and a tight-lipped mouth. She was not unkindly, but she was all busi-ness, a strict disciplinarian and a by-the-numbers teacher whose ultimate dream (I think, looking back) would have been to make us the classroom equivalents of synchronized swimmers, the pen-cils in our tiny hands moving as one across identically positioned sheets of paper. She called us "People" all the time and she was death on left-handedness. Her brother, she told us several times, worked for the New York Telephone Company and had advised her that the firm would absolutely not hire left-handed persons. Miss Arland made it clear that the New York Telephone Company was not alone in this regard and that any of us, then aged six, who had hopes of later employment had better be right-handed. Luckily I was, because it gave Miss Arland one less matter to chide me about. She never found much to praise in my pencil-manship, but at least it was done with the proper hand. Subse-quently I believe it was discovered that trying to change lefties

153

to righties brought on all kinds of traumas, but I was spared them, too.

The kind of rote-learning and constant drill Miss Arland believed in didn't leave much room for the free expression and creative play that got into education later. I probably missed a lot of fun, but I would like to think that the drills in spelling, reading, writing, and numbers have served me well.

Miss Zimmer cannot have been much older than Miss Arland, but she seemed grandmotherly by comparison. She was short and sturdy, with black hair and a rather sharp and prominent nose. She was more cheerful and easy-going than Miss Arland, although it may be that we simply needed less discipline in second grade, thanks to Miss Arland's stern guidance when we were in first. I have no recollections of riot or disorder. Actually I remember very few disciplinary problems in those elementary grades. It was school-school: no field trips, no audiovisual pleasures, sitting at the same desks except for gym and the lunch hour (most of us walked home). I can't think why we were as well-behaved as we were; possibly it was simply because we knew each other and played together. We didn't have to establish our images.

Miss Hamilton, May to her friends, had a great billowing pillow of snow-white hair. She could have played a sweet-faced grandmother in a magazine ad, although her true personality was of a slightly wispy and bemused great-aunt. My central memory of her class was of doing endless tall columns of addition and sheets of long division while she strolled up and down the rows, making soft clucking and cooing sounds as she glanced at our work. She was Miss Hamilton to the generations of Hammondsport citizens who had been her pupils and who would have thought it disrespectful to address her any other way. In retirement she was an indefatigable walker and appeared to be making continuous roundtrips between her apartment on upper Lake Street and the business section and the post office.

Teachers are always being described as bird-like (or perhaps

154

they used to be). But Mary van Etten did seem to be rather like a small, quick, bright bird who did nothing slowly. She was thought to be a real disciplinarian, like Miss Arland, but mostly she was just impatient to get on with it. Arithmetic was her forte, but she was one of those early teachers who encouraged me to write beyond the usual class assignments and who helped me to nurture my early suspicion that writing was what I eventually wanted to do.

The presumption, taken very seriously by school boards who did the hiring, was that women teachers could not be married and that male teachers *had* to be married. This invasion of private lives and free choice sits unpleasantly on the modern intelligence, reflecting as it evidently did some conscious or unconscious sexual fears. I suppose the surprise is that the teachers accepted the conditions without much struggle. A modern scientist might say that the women, in particular, had been conditioned from youth to accept that spinsterhood for teachers was the way it was, always had been and always would be.

Becoming a teacher amounted to a compromise of sorts, because teaching was one of the few professions open to women. And the fact of economic life was that it was a man's world and teaching was at least an honorable and respected way of making a living and achieving security (at very minimal levels).

For the women it was the price you paid for your social idealism, and your gender. There was no doubt that, whatever else was true, idealism was part of teaching and that women like Miss Arland and the others embraced the profession with a religious intensity and dedication. It didn't make the strictures against marriage any less cruel and short-sighted, but it underscored the fact that teaching was very much like a priestly vocation.

We students were luckier than we knew. Those grade school teachers had thirty children a year to whom they were substitute mothers or at least honorary aunts. Over their careers they had hundreds of children and yet it's not quite the same thing as the embracing warmth of kith and kin. So it is that whenever I drive

155

past the old stone schoolhouse where I began, I look at the windows of Miss Zimmer's homeroom on the Main Street side and Miss Arland's and Miss Hamilton's on the Lake Street side, and I hope that those women were in the end pleased by the choices they made for their lives. I also hope they guessed just how fondly and appreciatively they would be remembered.

The Making of a Reader

No one in my family wrote, but everybody read. My mother and both my grandmothers were heavy patrons of the Hammondsport Public Library, fond of the works of Faith Baldwin, Kathleen Norris and other romantic writers. We had no home library as such but there was a scattering of books, mostly quite old and origins mostly unknown. One of the few traces of my father after he left was his copy of Rafael Sabatini's *Scaramouche*. There was a copy of Henry Adams's *Mont-St.-Michel and Chartres* and several volumes of Thackeray, densely and forbiddingly printed. I've held on to some of them and *Henry Esmond* is on the long list of books I've promised myself to read one day. But in truth the books are mementos and like all keepsakes I value them for their power to evoke a particular past, simply by standing on a shelf.

I would have been thought odd in my family if I hadn't been a reader and the fact is that I can't remember when I couldn't read. I remember all too well learning to write: filling line after line of ruled paper with rows of capital letters and small letters and scrawling out long coils of O's and great thickets of up-and-down lines like snow fences. That comes back to me in all its boring dutifulness, along with the sharp voice of Miss Arland, insisting that I was capable of better. But was I drilled in sounding out the words, or in word recognition? Memory does not tell me. It seems to me that I have always been able to read, although this cannot be true, and that reading has always been the principal diversion of my life, which is true.

I had all the customary childhood diseases—mumps, measles, chickenpox, whooping cough and perennial heavy colds that arrived as regularly as the robins left. Except during the measles, which were said to be dangerous to the eyes and called for a darkened room, I used bedtime for reading. Someone gave me, or perhaps I inherited from an older cousin, a set of the "My Book House" volumes, which began with nursery-simple rhymes and advanced into more substantial stories and poems. The last time I looked the worn and tattered Volume One was still on one of our shelves, now bearing the crayon marks of two generations beyond mine.

I read hungrily and indiscriminately. I tore through the children's shelves at the Hammondsport Library in its first incarnation in the old stone schoolhouse (to which it has now returned, although in another part of the building). I met all the anthropomorphic toys and animals, dolls that lived and *The Little Engine That Could*. Cousin Caroline Champlin had preserved what seemed to be a complete set of the Bobbsey Twins series, and I walked across the valley to borrow them volume by volume. The Dohertys across the street had many of the Tom Swift series, and I absorbed them as well. I read the sports books of John R. Tunis, and I collected and read stacks of comic books and assembled long shelves of Big Little Books. It seems to me I followed Famous Funnies from its first issue and Superman almost as quickly. (I probably should have been a librarian because I loved having complete sets or series of magazines. But I married a librarian instead.) As with those secret decoder pins from the radio shows, I wish I had held on to an attic full of my youthful book and magazine collections; in the present market they would finance a long and comfortable retirement.

Miss Laura Ide Bailey, the town librarian, did her best to steer me onto the paths of literary righteousness, urging *Treasure Island* and the other classics upon me as soon as she perceived

I was ready for them. Now, naturally, I wish I had paid her even more heed than I did. I am still playing catch-up a half-century later. But I was then hot for more worldly and contemporary writings.

The Park Pharmacy was the place in town that sold magazines, from comic books to the *New Yorker* and all those now-extinguished voices like *Delineator, Liberty,* and *Colliers.* And in those last years before the paperback book came along and revolutionized the publishing business the Park had six wide shelvesful of pulp magazines. *G8 and His Battle Aces, Secret Operator 5, Dime Detective, Dime Western, Doc Savage, The Shadow:* it is curiously thrilling just to write down the names these decades later. There were others, *Spicy Detective* I recall in particular, that I glanced at on the sly but only once dared to buy. It was the first sexy reading I'd ever done. It gave me a very disturbing afternoon and I threw it in the furnace, not out of disgust but because I couldn't think of any entirely safe place to hide it.

I knew The Shadow, or Lamont Cranston (or Kent Allard, as he really was in the magazine, Cranston being only an intermediate cover), before I heard the radio show and Orson Welles's booming laughter about evil lurking in the hearts of men. It seemed to me that I already knew enough about the pains of writing to be astonished by the flow of words that emerged every other week from the man who called himself Maxwell Grant. A few years later I read Irwin Shaw's short story, "Main Currents in American Thought" (not then realizing that the title was an ironic re-use of the title of Vernon Parrington's book on American culture). Shaw's story was about the writer of a radio serial trying to churn out the next episode amid the distractions of family life, including the snarl of a vacuum cleaner. I thought instantly of Grant, trying to dream up new menaces for The Shadow while deadlines gnawed at his vitals.

If *Black Mask Detective* was on the shelf at the drug store I missed it. But later on, when I caught up with Dashiell Hammett, Raymond Chandler, and the hard-boiled writers of the Black

159

Mask school, I realized that my admiration for Maxwell Grant and The Shadow was well-placed. The swift narrative pace, the economy of the prose, the richness of invention, and the continuous excitement of the Shadow stories had its own kind of excellence, and Grant was another of the authors who was one of a generation that left something of a mark on the prose of later generations.

Having become a Shadow addict, I became a *Doc Savage* addict as well. The Man of Bronze, who had trace elements of Buck Rogers, Tom Swift, *and* a private eye, had a vivid cadre of trusted aides, including the dapper and adroit Ham Brooks and the brilliant but apish Monk Meyers. I see now, and may have perceived then, how useful for the author it was to have all those options for keeping the pot boiling and all those possibilities for getting Doc out of impossible scrapes.

I also read, a little less often, *The Spider* and *Secret Operator 5. Operator 5* was a strange and apocalyptic mini-series in print. Interestingly enough in the late thirties, the series envisioned the Yellow Peril invading the United States so that at last the President was hiding out in a cave or an underground redoubt where Operator 5 (who may even have been the President by then) was planning counterattacks against hopeless odds. On my interminable list of Things I Mean to Do When I Get Time is a project for retrieving Operator 5 from the archives, reading the stories again from the perspective of the 1980s and seeing exactly what they were saying and who was saying it.

Yet as much as I read in the pulps, they were only a part of my reading list (even beyond the school assignments). I had discovered the *New Yorker,* first out of my abortive efforts as a cartoonist, as I've said, but then for its short stories, profiles, criticism, and humor pieces. I decided that John O'Hara was the greatest short story writer in the world and that if I could write like him I would ask for nothing else in this life. I tried for years to write like him, in the same laconic and objective way, in which the dialogue told you everything that was going on inside the characters. But no one writes successfully like anyone else, and I had had no experiences that would easily translate into his spare style. (Later I saw that, like any writer, I'd have been far better off dealing with my own experience such as it was, in a voice of my own devising, instead of pretending to be an ancient cynical observer who has seen it all. But no one was at hand to give me that invaluable advice.)

I really did read almost everything. When I peddled the *Saturday Evening Post* I read it from cover to cover, which was its own kind of learning experience in those days. There were serials by Clarence Budington Kelland and Philip Wylie and William Hazlitt Upson and John P. Marquand (his Mr. Moto stories) and marvelous profiles by Alva Johnston and others. Ogden Nash was contributing his lovely silly rhymes to the Post Scripts page and I was fascinated to read the editor's notes about the various contributors, all of whom sounded peppy and uncommon. ("Charles Champlin, whose short story appears on page 00, plays the cornet and does his writing in a tree house he inherited from an eccentric aunt.")

Reading, it is obvious to me now, led me out of childhood and into adolescence and beyond. I learned a good deal about childbirth from Pearl Buck's *The Good Earth* and at least a little about romantic love at its most idealized from Ernest Hemingway's *For Whom the Bell Tolls* and *A Farewell to Arms*. I had joined the Book of the Month Club to acquire *For Whom the Bell Tolls*, not available locally, and I remained a member until I went in the Army, reading everything except the two-volume book dividend of Marcel Proust's *Remembrance of Things Past* which I still have and which is also on my list of projects I mean to get to. I acquired a whole shelf of books that you can't even give away to libraries because the book club made them so widely available—and because they were so often handed along to local libraries. I plowed through books, loyally, that passed out of mind almost as soon as I'd finished them. But I also discovered Arthur Koestler's *Darkness at Noon* and Jerome Weidman's *I*

Can Get It for You Wholesale, which led me to his other work. I read Samuel Eliot Morison's *Admiral of the Ocean Sea,* his magnificent biography of Christopher Columbus, and I began my discovery of the literature about the Civil War with *Reveille in Washington.* Propped in the window seat or draped on the wicker chaise longue in my bedroom, I acquired a kind of corollary education for which I have every reason to be grateful, and I am.

When what you are reading is wonderful it can be temporarily inhibiting to the would-be writer. There seems no hope of writing anything as fine, so you might as well give it up. But the ego is not that easily put down and soon enough you tell yourself that there is something else that needs to be written. It may be better or worse than what has gone before, but it will be different and it will be your own.

The more I read the more I wanted to be John O'Hara, Clifton Fadiman, E. B. White, Wolcott Gibbs, Alva Johnston, Ernest Hemingway, and perhaps even Samuel Eliot Morison all rolled into one. I set forth on various emulations, especially of what I thought of as the *New Yorker* style, which in my hands consisted of innumerable commas and an excessive use of the word "rather."

But soon enough I discovered that your own style emerges unbidden. If you are lucky it retains traces of the qualities you found in writing you admired—grace and clarity, precision and passion. If you are very lucky, what you write is not several people rolled together but is yourself, all in one piece.

Faith

Our house was a block down the street from St. Gabriel's Roman Catholic Church, a gray stone edifice with a steeple and a real bell rather than those ghastly electronic chimes that now play carols in season. St. Gabriel's is one of the four churches in Hammondsport. The Episcopal church, St. James's, is also built of gray stone. The Methodist and Presbyterian churches are of white clapboard in the clean and simple New England style. The Presbyterian Church had a beautiful steeple but lost it in a fire a few years ago and, such are the hard times of faith, has not yet found the funds to reconstruct it.

It was inevitable that my brother Joe and I would become altar boys at St. Gabriel's. There weren't that many Catholic boys of altar boy age who lived in town and could get to Mass and other services easily. But more than that our mother was a woman of a deep and abiding faith who found reassurance in the Church throughout her life. It used to worry me that she put a dollar in the collection when we had no money coming in at all. But she was a believer in bread on the waters and also in giving thanks for the help she felt she had had in coping with the divorce and with financial stress and then medical problems.

As I've said earlier, she played the organ at St. Gabriel's, often rising in the winter darkness to perform memorial High Masses at seven in the morning. She and the two regular singers in the choir, Millie Shaw and Jennie Canteloupe, would sometimes out-number the congregation. Her family, the Massons, had been pillars of St. Gabriel's from its early days. Their names were among those on the stained glass windows as donors, and Uncle Victor and his sisters were fixtures in the first two pews on the left-hand side. They always sat widely separated, as if to be alone with their thoughts and prayers. Aunt Julie sat at the aisle end of the front pew and was usually the first one at the altar rail for Communion. Aunt Tillie sat at the other end of the front pew and Aunt Josie and Uncle Victor sat in the second pew. They were tireless in their devotions although once, during a dull and interminable sermon by a visiting missionary who seemed to be going one by one through the natives he had converted, Uncle Victor arose and stormed out through the room beside the altar where we boys put on our cassocks and surplices. "I'm sorry," he whispered, "but I can't take another minute of that." I had always loved him, but my estimation for him that moment went skyrocketing up. Some things require more courage than others. His silent gesture was louder than a shout.

When Father Patrick J. Kelly, who had been the pastor as long as I could remember, finally retired, another Irishman, Father William Canaan, took his place and recruited a new crop of altar boys. Dick Lanphere and I as the tallest among us became the principal altar boys, flanking Father Canaan, and Joe and the younger boys served at the sides of the altar.

Another visiting missionary, a Paulist named Camillus P. Boyd, taught us how to say the Latin responses one afternoon, with a bowl of salted peanuts as our reward. Father Boyd was a huge, jovial man with a hearty laugh and manner and I'm sure that's why his name has stuck with me across the years. If I had been familiar with *Robin Hood* at that age, I'd have identified him with Friar Tuck.

There were more than Sunday Masses to be served. On weekdays when I didn't have school I would serve Mass, especially if it was a High Mass, for the soul of one of the faithful departed.

These were often forlorn, with Mother, Millie, and Jennie coping valiantly with the music, and Father Canaan and I the only males in sight. Then there were funerals and special observances called Forty Hours and week-long missions with a nightly ceremony called Benediction of the Blessed Sacrament which included the burning of incense (from the psalmist's words, "Let my prayer rise as incense"). And there was Lent, a wearying but (as I thought) purifying round of daily attendances and fasting that went even beyond the horrors of fish on Friday. Having to eat fish on Friday was for me one of the hardest aspects of growing up Catholic. Tuna salad sandwiches and tuna casseroles were the only two forms in which I found fish edible as a child. Lake Keuka trout and bass were said to be exquisitely tasty, but I had a fear of fish bones that equalled my loathing of pieces of eggshell in my scrambled eggs.

When the Church finally decided we could eat meat on Friday after all, I was not relieved: I was infuriated. I thought of all the guilt I had endured for my venal lapses (those furtive hamburgers) and all the battles I had had over pieces of fish that were not boneless no matter what anybody said. When I realized that it was all to no immortal purpose, my faith in the Faith was severely shaken. In its trivial way, the matter of fish on Friday was without doubt the first minor temblor, hardly registering on the theological Richter scale, of the deeper alienations that were to come.

Yet the positive side of growing up Catholic was very positive. The choir may have been reedy and occasionally off-key, yet High Mass and the other ceremonies—the incense rising in the light of the tall candles, the priests' robes handsomely brocaded, the cassocks red and the surplices starched and white—were wonderfully theatrical and inspiring.

Father Canaan, or any of the parish priests in those days, may never have been to Rome, may never have been outside the continental United States. But they and we were linked, if you thought about it at all—and I did—with an ancient past and with the whole world. Latin may technically have been a dead language, but it was universally alive in the Church and it made the rites at which I was an acolyte feel exotic, operatic, and mystical. Yet there was more to it than the theatricality. There was the feeling—once you had got past your grumbling resistance to waking up, getting out of bed, dressing, and plunging into the cold morning (it was always cold, somehow)—that you were doing something *good*. You were in the service of goodness, improving your character and working for the greater good and glory of God and the world. There was obviously something awfully smug and pompous about such considerations in a very young person, but I have no doubt I'm recalling them accurately.

What you gained as well, and probably more enduringly, was a feeling for mystery. Faith meant just that: *faith*. It said that there were things to be accepted for which there was no entirely rational explanation, no tangible, visible proof. The wine and water we altar boys poured over the priest's fingers into the chalice was indubitably still wine and water but it was understood to have become something more, just as the dry communion wafer was nothing so simple as a bland-tasting sliver of baked flour and water.

All altar boys at some moment imagine themselves as junior priests or as priests-in-waiting, I think. The priest you serve is both an authority figure and a role model. Unless he is a petty tyrant or cool and aloof (all priests are not created equal), he is a beloved and admired hero. As I entered into my teens I entertained now and again those almost universal speculations—fantasies in my case—about becoming a priest. I searched myself as best I could for signs of a vocation. There was never any direct family pressure or encouragement. But there was at least one sermon a year or a letter from the bishop read at Mass about vocations, and I always had the feeling it was aimed right at us altar boys. But by the time I began to think about the priesthood as more than a pretty fantasy, the possibility of making my way as a writer had taken hold of me. Even more damaging to the possibility of a vocation was my sense—early but accurate—that celibacy was not going to be within my powers.

But the magic hand of genetics is wonderful in its workings. Brother Joe, who is four years younger than I am, came to the altar as if he were coming home. One of the priests in our lives said years later that the quality of Joe's confessions when he was twelve left no doubt that he would become a priest and a fine one. My confessions never got much beyond the enumerations of "hells" and "damns." From early days I was guarded about what was really going on in my head, and unlike Joe or Mother I never found the confessional a place of reassuring dialogue and consoling counsel.

Joe was born compassionate. One night at supper he burst into tears because he couldn't finish his food and said he knew how many people were hungry in the world. I think we had just had a missionary visiting from one of what we would now call a Third World country. With exceptional maturity of purpose, Joe subsequently gave himself an ample taste of the secular world. He played competitive sports; he attended Andover (which became possible because I was by then being educated under the GI Bill); he spent two summers earning good money working on a railroad track gang; he attended Yale for a year. But in the end he had simply removed all doubts that he had a true vocation, and he has been proving it as a priest for more than thirty years. I envy him his serenity and his boundless capacity for selfless hard work.

What I prize most from a Catholic childhood is not the body of dogma learned by rote from the Baltimore catechism. I would have difficulty saying which articles of faith I believe or in what circumstances. But from those years I have held on to an acceptance of abstractions and metaphors, the use of images and symbols, and the poetic notion of inexplicable mysteries.

The anthropomorphic ideas of a white-bearded God and a red Satan with horns and a tail did not survive long under thoughtful scrutiny. Such conceptions surely had to be as mythic as Mother Nature or Zeus. Yet the notion of Otherness—of unexplainable, shapeless, intangible, immeasurable powers of good and evil—persists in me as in all but the most adamant and indefatigable atheists. The idea persists, it may be, only finally as an unanswerable question; but the question endures and is not yet to be confirmed or demolished by science.

It was dramatic and even romantic to grow up Catholic. It was also terribly hard, especially as you entered into those traumatic teen years when the fevers of sexuality were upon you. The wars of sin vs. purity raged within me, as I've said earlier, and if I was the battleground the terms of battle were those of the Catholic Church. If the loss of heaven and the pains of hell were not inhibiting enough (and for a long time they were), the fears of forfeiting innocence, purity itself, and the possibility of pride were more immediate and almost as potent as inhibitors.

I am quite ungrateful for having been so anguished a battleground of purity. I came to believe in later life that the strident stress on sex only as an occasion of sin (the bits about procreation were always in the fine print and not much discussed) had been distorting and even unhealthy. The subject took some re-learning.

Beyond the irresistible and distracting interest in sex, I fought a whole skein of self-doubts and apprehensions and, for quite a while, found solace in the Faith. For me the cool and lonely gloom of St. Gabriel's was frequently a restorative refuge on mornings after Mass or afternoons after school. There was a certain amount of self-dramatizing romanticism in these visits, and it seems to me I watched myself fondly as I knelt in supplication.

I never read deeply in religious texts, but the cadences of the Bible and of St. Augustine and St. Thomas Aquinas were inspiring to me as style as well as substance. (Years later one of the editors at *Life*, reading first drafts of my sonorous texts for picture essays, kidded me about my King James infirmity.)

I thought a lot about St. Gabriel's when Pope John Paul II

168

visited Los Angeles and set off a ceaseless round of ceremonies. Amid the motorcades and the gatherings and the incessant blitz of media attention, it did not take long to yearn for a little contemplative peace and quiet. I found myself remembering those movie scenes, more favored in the past than now, when the hero or the heroine—and occasionally even the villain—crept into the near-empty church and thought about things. Often he or she took courage and made hard decisions, there in front of the flickering candles. There was sometimes an elderly woman in a head scarf kneeling two or three pews back from the altar rail, saying her beads. (That might have been Anna Freidell, at St. Gabriel's.) Once in a while (usually unsuccessfully in dramatic terms) there was an echoing voice from the vaulted ceiling, offering guidance.

The church in the movies was almost always Catholic, not because the world was Catholic but because the visual adornment, the statues, the altar, the votive light, the candles, told you so quickly where you were and what you were supposed to know about what the characters were feeling.

The Pope's visit evoked a range of recollections in millions of us who made such visitations in childhood—who grew up in the church but whose present relation to it is a dotted line, if not an interrupted line. "You never break with Rome," a character says in one of John O'Hara's novels. What the character was suggesting, I think, was that the attraction the church held in childhood never entirely erodes.

The certainties, sometimes comforting, sometimes fearsome, of heaven and hell, sin, guilt, and forgiveness were indelibly received in childhood. So was the tidiness of the rituals, and their mysteriousness, and most of all the ideal of an achievable, sustainable purity. Far from least, in those days when the Latin was still used, there was indeed that feeling of timelessness and universality of which you were a part. You linked hands, symbolically, with ancient martyrs and contemporary citizens of all the world. I agreed with Evelyn Waugh and all the others who did not so much regret as actively resent the end of the universal

169

Latin. Like the lifting of the fish-on-Friday stricture, the reshaping of the rubrics and the language of the Mass betokened a larger incompatibility within me.

What the O'Hara character might have added is that you may not break with Rome but you may redefine the contract, whether or not you make the changes known to the party of the second part. It is clear from many recent polls that even among active Catholics there is considerable divergence between private practice and church doctrine.

The process of redefining where you stand and of setting your own theological terms in maturity is certainly not a Roman Catholic exclusive, but a more general life process. The rote-learned certitudes of the Hammondsport years—the textbook assurances about government, economics, parents, and education as well as religion—underwent a kind of trial by fire in the experiences of the grown-up years.

Faith itself has become a more personal matter, enriched (if that's the word) by an augmented faith in self. It is not always so. One good friend, a former Catholic, has turned to the far sterner certitudes of a fundamentalist Christianity which sets him a rigorous set of absolutes to believe and live by. Another friend is a militant atheist who (daringly enough) doesn't mind saying so on a bumper sticker. The friends seem equally happy in their divergent beliefs about belief, but equally adamant that they alone are right about things. Somewhere between are all those of us who cannot dismiss—or do without—that idea of Otherness, the concept of the Unmoved First Mover who or which (in what is the ultimate mystery) made the world.

The whirlwind appearances and the attending multitudes and the blizzards of press coverage when John Paul II was in Los Angeles produced a very mixed reaction in me. I felt a yearning nostalgia for those reassuring certainties of childhood, the fragments of altar-boy Latin, and the sweet-sharp aroma of incense rising like prayer. But I was also conscious again that very little

170

remains unchanged and that the easy serenity of my young faith had, like my Hammondsport itself, become largely memory, lovely and irretrievable.

Sex and Other Discoveries

Imagine that the quantity of sin in Hammondsport circa 1930–40 was about at the national average, which is to say there was a good deal of it. This has to be hearsay, because almost everything I knew about sex and other sins at that time was hearsay.

As I was growing up, the family not only expected absolute goodness but was at some pains not to let on that there could be falls from grace in the adult world. It was regarded as sinful in itself for the young to know about sin. My maiden great-aunts, my grandmother Masson, and my mother, who were the relatives I saw most of in my early days, had what I remember now as semaphore eyebrows, a secret communications system for dealing with things my brother and I were not supposed to hear or know about.

"How is dear Fannie Cameron?" one of the aunts might ask my grandmother.

"Much the same," my grandmother would reply, with a theatrically eloquent life of her eyebrows. Even then I understood that, Mrs. Cameron being in excellent health, the import of the eyebrowing was that Mr. Cameron, a large, soft man who was a minor foreman at one of the wineries, was either drinking again or philandering again or both again. I knew this from listening a lot to grown-up conversations when I was not thought to be

172

listening. Even then I may have been aiming for a career in journalism without knowing it.

"So sad about Emmaline Simms. Such a sweet girl," my grandmother might well say to the aunts.

"Yes," three voices would say as three sets of eyebrows rose.

Or it might be that only two sets of eyebrows would rise and one set would descend into a frown, indicating a puzzled lack of information. "What *about* Emmaline Simms?" the unknowing aunt would ask.

Now my grandmother and the other two aunts would tilt their heads imperceptibly toward me, eyebrows lifting quite slowly, for greater eloquence. What I had probably already heard elsewhere was that Emmaline Simms, who was unwed, was going to have a baby and everybody had a fair idea who the father was. (The joke, later found to be universal, was that Hammondsport never grew because every time a baby was born somebody had to leave town.)

I never let on that I knew what these cryptic signallings were about. But after a standing start, when sex was about twelfth on the list of the ten things I was most interested in, a feverish fascination with the subject took hold as it usually does. This was well before puberty and any possible operational interest in the subject. Long before it was anything more than an abstract subject for me, my curiosity was whetted by things my older pals said. In those circumspect days, before general circulation magazines dealt with sexual matters in intimate detail and "love" was the only four-letter word that books used, sex among the young was an item of myth, gossip, lurid exaggerations, and old husbands' tales. For me sex was an item of considerable confusion, not so much about the operational aspects of it as the emotional aspects of it and how it related to love. Love was white, vague, and distant as a cloud. Sex was dirty, furtive, and, often as not, pretty funny. The last operational confusion, which was how a woman could possibly give birth to a baby, was cleared up when *Life* magazine ran a controversial sequence of photographs in one of its early issues, which I studied with great and educational care. That left only the relation of sex to love to be understood and I'm not sure that I or the society have achieved full understanding about that yet. But that is another story.

Meanwhile back in Hammondsport there were lurid tales of conquests and heroic couplings, reports of nearby women (seldom named, however) who were allegedly of easy access and limitless appetite. Some of the older males who hung around the filling station would occasionally go off to adventures in brothels in Corning, Elmira, or Syracuse. I latterly suspect that their reports were as full of misinformation as the tales of acute nymphomania in North Urbana or Branchport. But even through the narrative nonsense (the guys at the station were nothing if not lively story-tellers) I caught what I can only call whiffs of disillusion, hints that the visits were not as much fun as they were expected to be. I still remember one of the proprietors of the station shuddering as he told about the utter boredom with which one of the ladies had received him.

I'm not sure that sex was an obsessive topic, but it was continuous and explorative. There was a lovers' lane in a small grove of trees at the lakeshore and the more daring teenaged boys used to hide in the shrubbery on summer nights and listen to and even creep up and spy on the action in the back seats. Some of the descriptions were so graphic they were probably partly if not wholly fictional, but they did make good listening. The Boy Scouts used to hold overnight camp-outs on the same beach and we would occasionally find evidences that safe sex had been practiced. These evidences of sin amidst the goodness of a Boy Scout camp-out were, if you wanted to think of it that way, perfectly symbolic of a larger struggle between innocence and badness.

All our sex talk existed in a kind of dynamic tension against the prevailing public morality. Ours was perhaps the next-to-last *non*-permissive generation. Sinful things happened but they were *understood* to be sinful. The notion of sin was as real as a speed limit. Sin and the ideal of purity were engaged in a kind of per-

174

petual arm-wrestle. The society thought so officially and I thought so privately. The fires in my own loins were fierce and eternal then as now, and while my life was too complicated to sum up easily, I think of those teenaged years as a constant, distracting, and exhausting battle between purity and indulgence. Purity kept winning because my awareness of sin and my capacity for guilt were inordinately large and powerful. I say this without particular pride and with some regret, because I've come to think that my strict observances made problems for me in later life. But that, too, is another story. Beyond the values purity undoubtedly has for its own sake, I'm sure I read more, studied harder, and exercised more as ways of sublimating those urgings, whether I knew it at the time or not.

As circumspect as the society was in those days there were nevertheless windows into the world of carnality. One year one of them turned out to be that venerable bucolic institution, the annual Steuben County Fair up at Bath. It claims to be the oldest in the country, dating from a race meeting in 1795. The sideshows in those days often included a musical revue (double-entendre songs featured). But one memorable fall the sideshows featured, along with the freaks and the strongman, a cautionary drama about the evils of dope and the young women whom drugs had led into lives of sordid commercial vice. Drugs were box office then as now. That year the Catholic pastor in Bath declared the whole fair off limits because of the dope show, but like all such prohibitions it only stirred up more excitement and attendance than there had been to begin with.

I attended the dope show. That year I was fourteen and looked eleven at best, but I sneaked in with some of my older pals. The show was crude and tawdry and topless. The only set was a brothel bedroom which was incessantly active, although the stage blacked out each time just before anything really incendiary took place. One man did treble duties as outside barker, master of ceremonies, and principal actor, leaping in and out of bed, and character, to continue his hellfire lecture about the dan-

175

gers of narcotics. He resembled an aging weasel, beady-eyed and lascivious to the point of parody. The girls, who ought to have been world-worn and hard, looked surprisingly young and pretty. When they looked at the triple-threat emcee it was with such undisguised and venomous contempt that the backstage dramas were probably more interesting than anything we saw out front. After the playlet there was for an additional quarter another performance in a rear tent, total nudity guaranteed in what the British call *les poses plastiques,* motionless displays that in England anyway got around the charge of being lewd acts. None of my group paid the extra to see the rest of the show. I'm not quite sure why, but it may have been that a stricter age limit was going to be enforced for the hotter stuff. I was as much relieved as anything else about leaving. I had watched the dope show with mixed emotions. It was another round in my internal struggle to stay pure in thought and deed. It was a guilty pleasure, to use a current term, and I had no trouble feeling both the guilt and the pleasure. But I also experienced a kind of shamed embarrassment on behalf of the women. You didn't have to be a premature moralist to guess that their lives were about as far from the glamor of show business as you could get. It was more outright nudity than I had ever seen, even without the revelations of the back tent, and I guess you could call the evening educational. It's just that it was impossible to separate the performance from the performers. I felt a shiver of loathing for the dirty old man and pity (mixed with erotic stirrings) for the women. Whether there were still further pleasures to be negotiated privately by the adult males after the plastic poses I don't know, although the gossip around the filling station was that there were. Either way the night seemed to me to be as close as I had yet got to the presence of carnal sin.

An eight-year-old in the present day might judge that I was unsophisticated and unworldly at fourteen; times do change. Yet we all had the basic biological information just about right. What we had wrong was thinking of women as objects of conquest and plunder rather than as partners. We were wrong about the real nature of love and it turned out to be painful getting it right.

Playboy and the other magazines like it were still a long way off. But there were clandestine equivalents with titles like *Paris Nights*, offering the same implied gospel of women as objects and featuring hot-breath stories and illustrations of super-pneumatic and sexually avid ladies. Those copies of *Spicy Detective* I used to read surreptitiously at the Park Pharmacy (and once or twice even bought) featured sleuths so continually distracted by voluptuous women that it was a wonder any crimes ever got solved. There were also, not commercially available but passed from hand to hand, pornographic books like the legendary Maggie and Jiggs cartoons and photo books thought to be scandalous, but no more explicit than those now sold at most metropolitan newsstands. In this desert of sleaze, not easily available, there was the *National Geographic* on proud display in every parlor and in which nudity was absolutely OK and educational in every way.

I read the sexy magazines when I occasionally, secretly could. But at heart I was a premature romantic and the heavier impressions on me were made by Hemingway's *A Farewell to Arms* and other novels of beautiful, doomed love. I should write a book called *I Was a Teenage Mess*, detailing not only the warfare between purity and sin, but between my dreams of romantic love and my stumbling efforts at sexual gamesmanship.

I was infatuated at eight (at a short-lived dancing class in the volunteer firemen's Hook and Ladder rooms). I was stricken with love at twelve (a new girl in school who looked like a Jon Whitcomb cover; alas she moved on all too soon). I survived an unrequited infatuation at fourteen and went steady for the first time, in an intense but chaste way, at sixteen. (Alas; I moved on and we met again, forty years later, as grandparents.) Living through these episodes, as a doctor might call them, in the Hammondsport years, I thought that the pain of growing up and confronting the onset of sexuality, thrilling and distracting as it was, was mine alone. But I saw at last that it belonged to all of us in the American thirties. And I came to see that we shared a common need, we men especially, to unlearn so much of what we thought we knew about sex and love.

Walter

Most of the news and feature stories carrying a Hammondsport, New York dateline in the last fifteen or twenty years have centered on that colorful maverick of the upstate wine business, Walter Taylor, and his Bully Hill Winery. Walter's epic confrontation with Coca-Cola in the years when Coke owned the Taylor Wine Company was the kind of big guy leaning on the little guy story that newspapers and magazines love. And Walter proved to have such a flair for publicity you'd have thought he had P. T. Barnum somewhere in his ancestry.

Walter's grandfather, also named Walter Taylor, was a cooper who founded the Taylor Wine Company in 1880. Old Walter's three sons, Fred, Clarence and Greyton, who was the present Walter's father, carried on the business and Walter himself, after a fairly footloose young manhood as an art student, finally joined the family firm.

The Champlins and the Taylors were friendly competitors for decades, with the accent on the friendly. The Fred Taylors lived diagonally across the street from us and they were Uncle Fred and Aunt Harriett—still another of my large collection of honorary aunts and uncles. The two families played bridge together, went to each others' parties and worked together on projects that benefited the whole town, like the restoration of the B&H after the flood.

179

My family's Pleasant Valley Wine Company had a twenty-year headstart and its champagnes had won some prestigious European awards. But the Taylors were shrewd merchandisers and after Prohibition their winery was able to remain privately held, in family hands, while Pleasant Valley went public to raise capital. In time, after the death of Uncle Charlie, who was the last of the Champlins to run PV, Taylor Wine bought Great Western, which had become the corporate name.

After the merger Walter—a burly, cheerful, gregarious, round-faced, moustachioed man who looks like a recently retired linebacker—and his father were given Great Western to run. Walter redecorated the executive offices, and there were rumors around town about one-hundred-dollar wastebaskets and other expensive accoutrements. But all went well until in 1970 at a meeting of wine distributors in San Francisco, Walter let fly an indicting attack on the way his own firm made wine.

He complained of the blending of local Hammondsport wines with bulk wines imported from elsewhere by tank car (indeed a standard practice), and about the use of chemical additives, and much else. The winery not unexpectedly fired him, Taylor scion or no Taylor scion. Walter and his father, who was known as "Spink" rather than Greyton, bought some vineyards just north of Hammondsport and started their own winery, named Bully Hill for the steep slope the vineyards were on. Walter's father died the next year, in 1971, and Walter carried on alone, vividly.

To dramatize his point about tank-car wines, he actually bought a well-used railroad tank-car and (no small feat of logistics) had it hauled to the site and mounted like a trophy on his hillside acreages. It is still there, a rusting monument to his point of view and his wizard promotional aptitude.

The Taylor Wine Company, which was at that point still owned and run by his family and lifelong friends, bit its corporate lip. Even as a child, Walter was known to be of independent, aggressive, and original mind. My mother, who worked for years as a teller in the Bank of Hammondsport (now the least

The entrance to the Pleasant Valley Wine Company (Great Western) as it looks today reflects a modern remodelling. The original structure was built in 1860. The winery had its own post office, called Rheims, N.Y., after the champagne capital of France.

branch of a vast conglomerate financial institution), came home one day to tell how Walter, then I suppose four or five, had visited the bank with his mother that afternoon, wandered through the president's office (the Taylor name carried certain privileges) and behind the scenes. He picked up a loaded .45 which, imprudently, lay on a shelf beneath one of the teller's cages. "Stick 'em up," Walter cried happily, the heavy weapon wavering in his small hands. It took several pairs of upraised arms and some nervous laughter to persuade Walter that the joke had run its course.

In 1977 Taylor Wine was bought out by Coca-Cola to become part of what the corporation called its Wine Spectrum. Coca-Cola, which over the decades has spent millions of dollars defending its trademarks, lost no time zeroing in on Walter. Although his own trademark was Bully Hill, Walter made sure the name Taylor was on his labels and in all his brochures. This was a natural reflection of his own not inconsiderable ego, but it was also very much an homage to his late father. Walter's lands adjoined his grandfather's original 1880 holdings, and from Walter's aggressive promotion of his name it was a reasonable inference that the sacred torch of wine purity had somehow passed directly from grandfather to grandson, bypassing the errant corporation up the valley.

In July 1977 Taylor/Coca-Cola brought suit against Walter for trademark infringement and unfair competition. The spectacle of a billionaire Goliath suing a millionaire David for what could be interpreted as unsportsmanlike conduct was irresistible copy. "The rebel prince of the vineyards," one headline called him.

Walter, who is now in his mid-fifties, is given to motorcycles and extravagant gestures. He started an FM radio station and put an airport on his hilltop property. He added a wine museum, a crafts shop, and a surprisingly good restaurant to his winery. He thinks of himself as being as much an artist as a vintner, and the wine shop at Bully Hill sells his prints along with other memorabilia. He has a special artist's status with NASA and is invited to attend launchings to do paintings. He is the last man in the world to take lightly an assault on his name and he made the most of his martyrdom.

In the first go-round, the Federal Circuit Court of Appeals ruled for Taylor Wine and against Walter. So Walter and his workers inked out the name Taylor on his labels and every other place it occurred, including the signs on the road in front of the winery, which he had named Greyton Taylor Memorial Drive in honor of his father. New materials were printed which incor-

Maverick's signboard has the name Taylor painted out as part of Walter Taylor's response to a court decision which prevented him from implying any connection between his Bully Hill and the original Taylor Wine Company which his grandfather founded in 1880.

porated the blottings-out part of the design. He posed some of his staff wearing masks as if to stress their namelessness. I stopped in at his winery restaurant for lunch one day late in 1979 and I counted forty-seven blots where the name Taylor should have occurred in the descriptive texts on the menu and nineteen more in a brochure given to winery visitors. The food was terrific and so was the wine and the view.

Walter appealed that first Appeals Court decision against him and a panel of judges agreed that that original verdict had been too sweeping. Coca-Cola later appealed, too, complaining that Walter had ignored the decision and had not mended his promotional ways. When the verdict on Coca-Cola's appeal came down late in 1979, it was clear that the Biblical tale of David and Goliath was only one of the analogies the press could draw upon. Walter could also be seen as the naughty boy who aims at the banker in the top hat but misses and hits a policeman smack in the kisser.

The federal judge found Walter and Bully Hill in civil contempt of the court. He reaffirmed the earlier decision and ordered Walter to pay court costs and to deliver all the offending labels and other materials to Taylor Wine for destruction. Walter, who occasionally signs himself "Artist and Poet" or "Artist and Freedom Fighter," circulated copies of the court decision to friendly journalists, asking, "Are we in America or Russia?"

But the order to deliver the materials to the winery was, I am tempted to say, tailor-made for Walter's gift for showmanship. He organized a funeral cortege, including a manure spreader in which to carry the offending labels, and it wound its noisy way down Bully Hill and through Hammondsport and up the valley to the Taylor winery, where an embarrassed foreman signed for the materials while other workers looked on from the windows and the roof.

I called Walter at the end of that year to see what his next move would be. He said he was thinking of changing his name to Walter S. Evil but hadn't quite made up his mind. (He later decided not to.) "I guess you have to love your enemy and laugh at yourself," Walter told me. "Still, I ought to be able to tell people who I am, historically."

One of the several ironies is that Walter's Bully Hill wines have been excellently reviewed over the years, and on their merits as well as their notoriety they sell briskly. Many of the tens of thousands of visitors to the Taylor Winery each year ask their guides, as a last favor, for directions on how to get to Bully Hill. There they tour Walter's winery, visit his wine museum and gift shop, inspect the tank car, have a bite at his restaurant, and admire the sweeping view of Keuka Lake.

While the legal fireworks appear to be over, Walter's gift for promotion still flourishes. Once each summer he treats the cottagers around the lake to a truly dazzling fireworks display at the winery, visible from miles away. He also holds an annual sleep-in ox roast which draws visitors from a wide area and is regularly sold-out. He has combined it with a goat show, which evolved from one of his ripostes to the legal battles. He made the rhetorical point that while the courts could get his name they could not get his goat. Pursuing this thought led Walter with impeccable logic to holding an annual goat show on his premises, at which as many as a thousand prize animals are reportedly on view.

It is another irony that Coca-Cola, having won its expensive legal battles with Walter, subsequently quit the field, selling most of its wine operations, including Taylor and Great Western, to Seagrams. Before the sale was announced, there had been rumors in the industry that Coke was going to close both of the wineries because of declining sales. Seagrams ran the wineries for a while but toward the end, to the horror of local oenological purists, was primarily making the newly-popular wine coolers. Most recently Seagrams sold the wineries to a management group called Vintners International, which has vowed to emphasize New York state wines. (Coca-Cola had concentrated its wine advertising on its Taylor California Cellars brand, ignoring the Hammondsport brands completely.)

No one is harassing Walter any more, but he continues to keep things stirred up. He has evolved from being a maverick to being a maverick elder statesman. He still chides the big wineries on the way they make wine; he issues a price list pointedly demonstrating that he pays better prices to local grape-growers than the big fellows do; he has made himself a spokesman (self-appointed but very audible) in the cause of New York state wine.

The last irony is that Walter's Bully Hill operation now looks as much in the mainstream of the wine business as his grandfather's vision for Taylor Wine did in 1880. The trend in the Finger Lakes wine-growing areas increasingly since World War II has been toward the formation of boutique wineries—small operations run by an individual, a family, or a small group more interested in quality than quantity.

The Davids proliferated while the Goliaths were having their troubles with competition from both California and French wines, compounded by the difficulties of absentee corporate ownership and direction. Under their new owner-managers, Taylor and Great Western have a good deal of local autonomy once again, and sales of their champagnes in particular are growing fast. But there is also no doubt that the maverick poet-artist of Bully Hill has had a satisfying time of it, if not quite the last laugh.

Labor Day

On the first day I lived and worked in Southern California I saw Katharine Hepburn double park her Thunderbird on a Beverly Hills street and run into her bank in a green slack suit that appeared to be made of silk, and I thought what a long way Southern California is from Hammondsport, New York. I am still not entirely accustomed to the differences: the flowers in bloom and the grass green all year long, the hot, dry, dangerous winds and the earthquakes, the palm trees and the infrequency of rain. There are seasons but, except for the rain itself when it comes at the turn of the year, they are so subtle you have to live here for years to identify them (spring is morning fog).

More than in most regions the great holidays define the year. But they, too, are different. I've never quite grown accustomed to hot Christmases when you can splash in the ocean and work on a tan. Yet it is Labor Day and not Christmas that has been most transformed for me by the dislocations of weather, age, and social change. Growing up in Hammondsport, Labor Day was the heaviest punctuation of the year for me—a rite of passage that was melancholy to the point of bleakness, even if the sun beat down gloriously, as it usually did.

Keuka Lake is lined with cottages (shoreline frontage now goes for a thousand dollars a foot, friends say). And it was on Labor Day weekend that the summer visitors closed their cottages. The summer people were part of the excitement of growing up in Hammondsport. The girls from away looked more beautiful and sophisticated and, in season, sexier than the local girls. The local girls thought much the same things about the summer boys. Most of the cottagers came back every year and on Fourth of July weekend there would be reunions in the park at Hammondsport and around the docks at Keuka and Lakeside and at the skating rinks that night. The college crowd, which I used to watch with a terrible wistfulness, sailed together and drank together at the Keuka Hotel and Snug Harbor and Bakers on Lake Salubria in Bath, which had a small dance band, and at country taverns. They wore white to show off their tans and I think they were all, the men and the women, very conscious of being young and beautiful.

But then it was Labor Day weekend and the summer visitors closed their cottages. The essential rituals have not changed in a half-century, although more of the cottages are now year-round homes. And there is a kind of ceremonial display of fireworks around the lake on that weekend, a flashy farewell to the summer holidays. The sails come off the sailboards, masts are lowered, and boats lifted on hoists in the boat houses or put on trailers for a winter's stay in the garage at home. The big purring Chris-Crafts take a last spin down the water and the lake is restored to the care of the local fishermen whose boat lights you can see bobbing in the night like slow fireflies. The skating rinks, built on pilings over the water, were terrifically romantic when there was moonlight on the ripples (and when there wasn't). But on Labor Day weekend the public address systems played the organ recording of "Goodnight Ladies" for the last time and the shutters would be lowered and locked for the long winter.

Starting Saturday noon the summer cars, untidily loaded with kids, wet bathing suits, and bags, would move in a slow procession around the square, heading home to Corning, Elmira, and Rochester.

188

Labor Day Saturday night was, of course, the last performance in the park by the town band, and even before I joined the band I thought the concert was the centerpiece of the whole weekend. The adults still parked around the four sides of the park, honking their horns as applause, and the little kids ran around the bandstand playing noisy tag-like games that had no rules and no end. The teenage girls strolled around in clusters of two or three and the boys strolled in their own clusters, usually slightly larger, four or five. They were protected by the numbers from their own shyness, but there was usually a leader, bolder than the rest, who did the talking to the girls. Once or twice I trailed along with the male clusters, hoping for clues on how to talk to girls. But all the joshing and heavy-handed teasing when the clusters met struck me as very foolish and to no point. I still didn't know how to talk to girls, but I had an idea how not to.

The concerts always felt like scenes from a movie, with a romance or a drama happening somewhere in the crowd. I used to walk in the crowd, imagining I was in a movie. Sometimes I was just a sort of spectator-commentator, an adolescent Somerset Maugham or John O'Hara observing the human comedy for later stories. (This was from my aloof, inscrutable period.) At other times, and most keenly on Labor Day weekend, I was no longer the witness—I was the protagonist, the boy-man about to meet or to find again the girl-woman of his dreams. On that night it was probably to have a tearful farewell, ripped apart by destiny until the following summer. The brassy, reedy music of the band, mellowed out by the night and the trees, was a perfect underscoring for the drama in my imagination. Later, when I joined the band there was still a movie in my mind; all that had changed was the part I was playing.

That last Saturday really was a night of goodbyes, discussions of the horrors of school that lay ahead, and the impossibility of learning geometry, Latin, or chemistry. There were promises to write, almost never kept as I remember. It was a foretaste of a life's-worth of farewells, some more irrevocable than others. Even the melancholy sounds idyllic and I expect it was. The excitement didn't cost much which was just as well, because money was still tight. But the B&H was running again, champagne was being shipped, and gasoline was no worse than a quarter a gallon. If you were young and discovering girls and Hemingway and Artie Shaw and Humphrey Bogart, it was possible to set the war news from Europe aside and taste the moment (flavored as it was with Grimaldi's milkshakes and cherry phosphates at the drug store).

It was particularly clear on so perennial an event as Labor Day Saturday night that there really was a continuity in Hammondsport time, a flowing from past to present to future—a promise of continuity. The last strains of summer echoed through the September air as the band concerts commenced at the turn of the century. The young partings might have been sweet sorrow, but you had to believe that beyond the snow and the algebra there would be other confident summers.

Thanksgiving

Childhood is terribly short, no more than a dozen years long at most, a half-dozen years that can be remembered with any clarity before the shifting of gears takes you into adolescence. But memory, that most mystical instrument, has a way of telescoping several Thanksgivings (the day I have in mind) into a single composite picture and then multiplying the composite until it appears to stretch endlessly into time, like an image in a hall of mirrors.

I can't say with any accuracy at all just how often Mother and Joe and I went to the Masson house for Thanksgiving dinner. Yet memory translates a relative handful of times into always, and I hold almost no other early recollection of the day, except at the house on Vine Street, with Uncle Victor at the head of the table, doing the carving.

We were never an enormous number around the table, a dozen at most, presuming Aunt Lucie Carpenter was still in town after overseeing the grape-picking in her late father's vineyards and had not yet returned to California for the winter, and if an old family friend, Aunt Fannie Larrowe from down Vine Street, had been invited. There were otherwise Uncle Victor's three sisters, Aunts Julie, Tillie and Josie, my grandmother Nano Masson, Cousin Melanie Masson and Aunt Leila Masson, whose late husband was a cousin of Uncle Victor and the aunts.

There was a solemn grace, then a clear soup, and then what seemed a ballet of plate-passing and dish-forwarding. The adults had sparkling burgundy, which Uncle Victor himself may have made at Taylors or Pleasant Valley (he consulted at both wineries). Joe and I were not included in the wine drinking. Great-grandfather Jules Masson and his wife had preserved many a European attitude in America, but wine for the children, even watered wine, was not one of them.

Joe and I were served first and usually allowed to start right away, with frequent interruptions for the dish-passing. It became a small annual joke in a family that loved small ritual jokes that when Uncle Victor had loaded the last plate with turkey and stuffing and handed it on, he said, "Seconds, anyone?" At least once Joe and I had eaten so fast we had cleaned our plates before Uncle Victor had sat down to begin his meal. The rest of the ritual consisted of cries, led by my grandmother, that Uncle Victor should be allowed to sit down and eat something first.

One of the Hammondsport legacies that has hung on into my present life is that, having myself become the carver of the Thanksgiving turkey, I ask, "Seconds, anyone?" as I hand around the last plate. Or, if I don't ask it quickly enough, one of my now-grown children will say, teasingly, "Seconds, please, Uncle Victor." They have heard about the ritual from my childhood and they love it and have extended the tradition in memory of a small precise man with pince-nez glasses whom they never knew. The truth is Uncle Victor had it fairly easy. With six children of our own, plus spouses and grandchildren, we have been as many as twenty at the table (or tables) and I've legitimately been asked for seconds before I sat down. I don't mind at all and neither, I realize now, did Uncle Victor.

I've wondered in recent years just when it was that Thanksgiving ceased to be Thanksgiving only and became the first day of Christmas, the carols having invaded the radio commercials even before the turkey was carved, and the traffic jammed and the shopping malls mobbed the day after the cranberry jam went down.

Thanksgiving may already have been a launch pad for Christmas shopping when I was a child, but I was luckily unaware of it. And in those nonaffluent late-Depression days I don't believe it was. Back then Thanksgiving stood on its own, a blessed breather to keep your spirits afloat between the end of summer and Christmas.

In those years you could still have bonfires with a clear conscience, and the indoor smells of the Thanksgiving food are pleasantly mixed in memory with the sharp aroma of burning leaves. The weather was usually clear and snappy, ideal for tossing a football around for a while to settle all that turkey and fixings, while the adults were sentenced to conversation in the living room; I think they envied Joe and me in the restorative tangy air.

Second only to Christmas, Thanksgiving is, as it was then, the holiday that has resisted the tendency to become just another free day, without real meaning. It hangs on to its originating spirit. In upstate New York the pilgrim past was near at hand geographically but it also felt close historically, because yesterday did have a way of persisting into Hammondsport's todays. The specifics of thankfulness were different in the thirties than later. Even in austere times, there was reason to be grateful for simply having survived and, having survived, to be living in a realistic hope that there would be better days.

As children we could not be unaware that we were living in hard times, even though we couldn't sense the depth of the adults' concerns and frustrations. In the way of children, we could be thankful and then complacently eat ourselves silly. Complacency is harder to come by these days. There may be an overlay of affluence that did not exist when I was growing up in Hammondsport, but the overlay grows more transparent all the time. Unless you live in a sealed house and do not read, listen, watch, or think, you cannot be unaware of the homeless, the un-attended sick, the wretchedly educated young who belong to an apparently permanent underclass which is not limited by race, creed, color, or geography, but which is united by hopelessness.

Almost as cruel—because it represents the death of hope and confidence—there is the shabby genteel poverty of the men and women who thought they had provided for their golden years, having worked hard and saved and been, as they imagined, prudent. Instead they have inherited a pinched existence on fixed incomes. They surface briefly in the newspapers when they are evicted from properties that are being converted to yield a higher rate of return from younger and better-off tenants or buyers.

Uncle Victor is long gone and so is everyone else who sat at those Thanksgiving dinners in Hammondsport except my brother Joe and myself. Yet I find curious parallels between the celebrations of a half-century ago and now. It was hard then not to be aware of the gap between the haves and the have-nots; it is even harder now. In fact, I can't help thinking that Thanks-giving is ready for a new focus, addressed not to those who have much to be thankful for, but to those who don't. Actually it would be less a new focus than a re-focus, a return to the share-the-blessings spirit that, if the schoolbooks were right, launched the holiday in colonial times. Amid all the concern about home-lessness as the terrible blight on the face of America, I can't help thinking about my friends, the economic nomads of the Depres-sion, bouncing in and out of Hammondsport in search of some small foothold on security.

In many ways, the world in which I stand to carve the turkey is unimaginably different from Uncle Victor's. (I can't envision what he would have wanted to watch on television unless it was the occasional opera and some National Geographic specials.) But as I think back over all my Thanksgivings, the linking theme between then and now and the prime reason for thankfulness is having the family at hand, watching the carver pretend to be Un-cle Victor.

194

Christmas Past

It is easy to summon the story-book aspects of the Hammondsport Christmases—walking up a hill road called the Winding Stairs with my friend Joe Eade to cut a tree in the woods, being bedded down early and then awakened for Midnight Mass (standing room only, the aroma of spiked eggnog in the congregation competing with incense from the altar, the once-a-year visitors dozing off in the heat in the rear pews.)

A curtain divided the living room from the dining room where the tree stood, and after church my brother and I were allowed to have one small present each to tide us over until morning. It was a great disappointment to have chosen one of what Dylan Thomas in "A Child's Christmas in Wales" called the useful presents, wool socks or utilitarian mittens or a scarf as rough as sandpaper.

One Christmas I was sick and our tree was installed in my bedroom. Uncle Victor's present that year was an ancient wooden tool chest full of perfectly maintained tools of wonderful Victorian quality. Dr. Kuhl, our family doctor, paid a Christmas Eve call but I was already asleep. He was prevailed on to carry the tool chest up to my room. I stirred and came halfway awake while he was in the room, thinking I'd heard something. The doctor had to crouch at the foot of the bed until he was sure I had drifted back to sleep. I hadn't a clue as to how to use any

195

of the tools constructively, but I wish I had them all now; they were a treasure beyond my grasp. Those were the years of the heirloom presents, sometimes known in the clothing line as hand-me-downs: fancy sweaters, only a few sizes too large, from an uncle who was renewing his wardrobe, a bathrobe, floor length on me, from another uncle and, more enduringly, a complete set of Dickens inscribed but not read (I judge from the uncut pages) by a great-aunt long gone and handed along by Aunt Tommy, my father's sister.

Christmas, it seemed to me, was when it was so cold that the hairs in your nose stuck together, frost formed on the scarf over your nose and mouth and the snow underfoot did not crunch but squeaked unpleasantly to the ear, a close cousin to the sound of fingernails crossing a blackboard. The mercury, as they used to say upstate, would hang three clapboards below the bulb. Even after a quarter-century of California Christmases, there is still something entirely *illicit* about being able to be warm outdoors on that day. It is as if you should pay for your presents with watery eyes, chapped hands, and maybe even a touch of frostbite. Christmas by the sunny sea does have its own appeal. It falls in the rainy season and if indeed there has been rain and then sunshine the hills go overnight from dead brown to the soft green of springtime and there is a sense (more appropriate to Easter, probably) of the world, having been cleansed, renewing itself. Then again, the Christmas trees, ten dollars a foot in Southern California, quickly dry out on the sunbaked lots and the reindeer on view at the shopping malls are subject to heat prostration. It is no use observing that the seasonal climate in California may be very like the weathers of the first Christmas in the Middle East. The holiday has acquired a sub-Arctic overlay from its Western European origins, and that's that.

Holidays breed memories, bringing the past forward into the present so you can think about it with regret or relief and usually some of both. Of all the holidays Christmas is always the most fraught with memories for me, but in a warm climate they sneak up on you unawares, as if your subconscious were still waiting for the snow and freezing cold. The memories escape unbidden from the unlit and cluttered closet of the past, a tangle of the trivial and the important which I can't sort out. For instance I see and can almost feel the brown corduroy trousers, washed until they had gone soft as a dish-rag, that I was wearing the year I fell and sliced open my knee when we were bringing home the tree. I see—and can't think why—the red paint covering the runners of new sleds. It was to prevent rust but it meant that the first thing you did if you got a new sled was to drag it along a bare sidewalk with a rider aboard to grind off the paint. A sled hardly slid unless the runners were bare and shiny steel.

The fact that by the fortunes of fate my father died on Christmas has ever since left the day shadowed with melancholy. I think of his messed-up and foreshortened life and it's hard to escape contemplations of my own mortality. These Christmas mornings I am surrounded by three generations of my life and I'm doubly aware of both the preciousness and the fragility of life.

It seems to me I can remember the feeling, almost the moment, when I crossed that invisible line between pure childhood and the pains of sophisticated knowledge. It fell in that one tremulous and terrible season when you had to *pretend* not to believe in Santa Claus even though, against all rationality and the pressure of cynical friends, you still did believe in Santa or wanted to desperately.

The same Christmas memories play differently as your years go on, like unpredictable reruns that change their plot lines after their first appearances in prime time. The merrier and more affectionate Christmas is as you watch your children and their children move into maturity, the more the day is visited by Christmases past and by the felt but unseen presence of family members and friends who once were part of the day and are no more. Watching the tearing-apart of the Christmas wrappings, I feel miles and years away and have to shake myself back to present laughter, seeing some part of me in the grandchildren who are only now stockpiling their memories of the day.

I've celebrated Christmas in many different places—almost a dozen houses, I suppose. In 1944 I was in Southampton, England, trying to stay warm in a tent in freezingly cold weather while we waited to cross the Channel on LSTs, and I remember walking past the cathedral on Christmas Eve and hearing a sudden swell of music as the door opened to admit a late-comer. I wondered if the altar boys had the same trouble lighting the high candles that I used to have. I wanted to stop, but I was due back at the encampment and I walked on.

Despite that Christmas memory and all the others of different places and different times, I am at last always back in Hammondsport, anxious to have all the family observances over with—even the turkey dinner—so I can assemble my small treasures like a miser and gloat over them (if they were gloatable, and some years were better than others). After a while toward late afternoon the family ties would begin to bind a little too tightly and I would wander into the street, hoping to run into Justin, Ward, Sonny, Howard, Dick, Roger, Pete, Richard, or John William and see what the day had brought them.

Everybody complains about the commercialization of Christmas and I have, often and loudly. But the spirit of the season remains so indefatigably strong that all the huckstering can't destroy the deep satisfactions of generosity—the giving and the receiving. Deciding which drug store perfume Mother might like best is a very early memory, along with trying to make the Christmas tree lights work. And one of the rewards of parenthood is watching your children to see the tearing, competitive greed of Christmas morning gradually replaced by the dawning realization that it is as much fun (almost, anyway) to give as to receive.

Re-experiencing the now-distant Hammondsport Christmases through grown-up eyes I appreciate that in those Depression years the holiday was an oasis of cheer and the hope of better

198

times, set amid the grey uncertainties that matched the standard weather. It is clear to me now that Christmas was more cost-efficient in those days, with handmade presents and cards and the redistribution of family treasures making do for an under-supply of dollars and reflecting instead an abundance of thought-fulness and ingenuity.

"The past," L. P. Hartley says at the opening of his novel *The Go-Between*, "is another country. They do things differently there." And so they do, or did. And when the holiday gatherings thrust me back in memory to Hammondsport (I am occasionally helped along by a cold and knifing wind out of the foothills) I tell myself that many things, back there where the past was, were worth keeping.

Generations

Once several years ago when I was a magazine correspondent and had a little spare time and energy to try my hand at fiction I began a short story, but then abandoned it because I couldn't imagine where it went or how it ended. A quiet but powerful emotional moment had sent me back to my Hammondsport days, remembering not the pleasures but the pains.

The story was actually less a story than a vignette in which I wanted to recapture the rush of feeling I had had one evening as I looked down on my sleeping son, who was then, I suppose, not quite two. He looked very much like some pictures I have of myself at the same age, and it seemed to me there were a million things I wanted to tell him that I had learned over the years and that would spare him pains and embarrassments of large and small magnitude. But I knew that I wouldn't be able to tell him those million things. I probably couldn't spare him even the most trivial of chagrins. He would have to learn the hard way, as we all do. So what I had felt that night, standing beside the crib, was a kind of fond helplessness.

We were then living in Chicago and I was in my mid-twenties, but looking at him I saw myself back in Hammondsport in those same life-shaping years he was entering. He would never have the Hammondsport experience and I wondered how different his young life would be. If he looked like me it was possible he would grow up like me, which meant that after the pink plumpness of babyhood he would be pale and skinny to the point of scrawniness. But he wouldn't have that covey of maiden aunts and widows fussing over him, worrying about his paleness and urging him to acquire rosy cheeks, as if it were within his power. My cheeks were never rosy and it was years before I could even get a good tan. On the other hand he would never enjoy the keen and loving interest of his aunts (his great-great-aunts, actually), or laugh at their small, schoolmarmy jokes. (Aunt Tillie used to chant, "Can you see, can you sigh, can you Con-stan-tie; can you nople, can you pople, can you Constantinople!") He would have only the vaguest, briefest memories of his grandmothers and he would never know what he missed.

At two it was no use forewarning him that his thinness would one day be a fond, nostalgic recollection, as my thinness already was—a state of body to be remembered, forlornly, while riding an exercise bicycle or rejecting dessert.

No use to tell him never to forget his handkerchief. It is a lesson that is not well learned until you have sat through second-grade arithmetic with a runny nose and a short-sleeved shirt and *no* handkerchief, in an agony of snuffling humiliation. Then that cautionary lesson, like most lessons, is self-taught.

Watching young Chuck sleep I couldn't then be sure if he would be better coordinated than I was. If he was going to be as clumsy as I had been with bats, gloves, baseballs, basketballs, volleyballs, stilts, parallel bars, jungle gyms, and anything else connected with being able to tell your muscles what to do, then there was nothing I could do to lessen the sting of those small, hard failures from the school years when the athletes reign supreme. There was nothing wrong with me organically; it was just that I never seemed able to make the right physical moves two times in a row.

But even if your athletic skills are laughable, I would have told him, try your hand at sports, because on those rare times when the hook shot slices through the net, the fly ball drops into the glove after the long chase, or the winning run scores on your fluke single over third, then the joy is all the more sensational, because it is so astonishing and unexpected. Even now I can re-live each of those infrequent triumphs in my life: the running catch in the pick-up game at Dick Para's farm, the basket (a one-hand push from the side) in the Jay Vee game, the single in the American Legion playoff at Bath. I can count the moments on one hand, but nobody's counting except me anyway.

What it seemed to me I learned at Hammondsport was that the early school years belong to the natural athletes, not the good spellers or memorizers or the budding writers. The scholars' moments of glory, if there are to be any, will come later. It's just that it's easier to understand all that when you're looking back than when you're there.

There were scholar-athletes at Hammondsport as elsewhere and one of the best in my day, Fred Sprague, made it to a Dodger farm club for a season or two and then went on to a fine career in business until he died, far too young, in the crash of a company plane on a hillside above Hammondsport. A different kind of sadness surrounds the high school athletes who were not good enough for the pro ranks but who had nothing else going for them and whose lives hit their high points, symbolically, in the regional playoffs in Alfred, New York. There were the non-scholar athletes among my friends at Hammondsport, too. I think of two or three of them whenever I re-read Irwin Shaw's short story, "The 80-Yard Run," about the college athlete whose later life is an anti-climax. Shaw's athlete had lied to himself about the eighty-yard run, so even the memory doesn't hold up while he sells men's clothes from campus to campus. For my high school pals the sports glories were real enough; it was just that nothing followed except workaday jobs.

I thought, that night in Chicago, of all the things you have to suffer through in your young years, everything from bad skin to minor betrayals, from the first time you experience death near at hand to the possibility of moving away from everyone you

202

know and love, from being miserably shy and tongue-tied to being scared in any of the ways the world can scare you in peacetime or war.

There would be pleasures to look forward to, of course, some of them immense, like the excitements and the enduring satisfactions of real love. If I wasn't thinking of them that night it was because I was seeing my son's vulnerability, even as he smiled in his sleep. It would have been a way to end the story, on a note of vague hope—if I had felt secure enough to imagine a happy ending.

The night in Chicago and the vignette I tried to write came back to me with great clarity a quarter-century later, on the day my son got married. I did a quick calculation and realized he was that day almost exactly the same age I had been the night I watched him sleeping. During the wedding ceremony I kept remembering the traumas we had been through, including a Sunday afternoon in White Plains a few years later when a neighbor came up the street carrying him, bloody and dazed after he'd been hit, accidentally, by a baseball bat. For a terrible moment I was sure he was dead or dying, but he has only a faint scar (now almost invisible) to show for the scare of a lifetime.

Chuck survived the paleness and the thinness and even the wearing of glasses, a trauma I'd forgotten about, but which had been an awful trial to me when I'd first had to wear them at age nine. By some genetic kindness Chuck inherited a degree of coordination I never enjoyed and put it to the severest test, hang-gliding in his pre-marital years. He obviously skipped the acrophobia, or fear of heights, which was one of the embarrassing inconveniences of my childhood. I had had to write off some of the pleasures of a Hammondsport childhood, like diving from the boathouses and climbing the steeper falls in the glens. The matter of heights, a problem that did not really end with school, was still one of those difficulties that made me eager to grow up and get on.

I have always liked somebody's line that the best way to recall a happy childhood is to have a bad memory. That night in Chicago I could have recited a whole litany of childhood pains and insecurities. I thought my head was too large and my neck too small and I imagined that I looked top-heavy. I worried that my ears were too large and was only slightly consoled by the news that Clark Gable's ears were also regarded as too large. I worried about thinness, paleness, wearing glasses, and being afraid of heights, and later by pimples and a false alarm that I was losing all my hair prematurely. I collected inadequacies the way others collected matchfolders. I overdressed from an early age, imagining that the shirts, ties, and jackets concealed my scrawniness. In high school I even wore ascots, the better to disguise the true circumference of my neck. All I really achieved was a reputation for being thin but dapper. To this day I feel alien in jeans and open shirts. (A cynical friend says we all dress for the period at which we peaked, and there may be something to it.)

What I really wanted to convey to my sleeping son that Chicago night was the idea that it all passes. There may be other peer pressures later on, but none are quite so tough and so *inescapable* as the pressures in early school. Then, so I realize looking back, the things that mattered were things you couldn't change. But sooner or later you begin to be able to make more of your own choices, to design your own running. With a little luck, you can attend to your strengths and stop being obsessed by your shortcomings, which may at that be real, imaginary, or temporary.

At a dinner party in Chicago a few months before our son was born a spinster friend with a wry sense of humor said, "It always seems to me that the toughest part of being a parent would be figuring out how to pass on your hard-won wisdom to your children without incriminating yourself so thoroughly that they throw you out of the house." As I came to see, there was a good deal of wisdom in what she said. What saves us, I suppose, is that so many hard lessons have to be learned but can't be taught, so we're spared a little self-incrimination at least.

204

Whatever his own painfully acquired lessons are, Chuck is stuck with them, as Katy and John and Judi and Susan and Nancy are stuck with theirs, and Peggy and I are stuck with ours. Wisdom is self-induced and all the homilies about patience and compassion and sharing and forgiveness only become home truths after they have been proved in the fires of experience.

Impossible to tell a waking child, let alone a sleeping child, that there is still no substitute for hard work, but nothing so satisfying as the results it can produce. You do what parental steering you can: urging the long view, for example, and insisting that some things are more important than others and that some temporary gains aren't worth it. But then it turns out that the most influential thing you've done is live your own life to your own standards. You have been watched when you didn't know it.

I remember Shirley Booth in *The Time of the Cuckoo* on stage remarking in that cracky voice of hers, "As my mother used to say, enjoy yourself; it's already too late." By the time it occurs to you to give general guidance it is probably already too late. That rush of memory and good feeling I experienced on a Saturday afternoon in Pasadena, watching our son dancing with his beautiful bride, was in effect the happy ending to that distant and unfinished vignette in Chicago a quarter-century earlier. It was also the beginning of a new long story and a reminder of the continuity of life. At the wedding, I noted that Chuck and I had both remembered our handkerchiefs.

Now, another decade later, Chuck and Theresa have a first son of their own and it is Chuck's turn to gaze upon his sleeping son Alexander and conjure up a list of the things he would spare him, if he could.

Leaving

It never really occurred to me that I might one day move away from Hammondsport permanently. I imagined that if all went well I would somehow go off to college, but then I would come home again. Even as the idea of becoming a writer took hold of me I was sensible enough to know it would be a long time before I could support myself with a pen, if I ever could. But in my handsomest fantasy I saw myself working at the Cellar, as we called the winery, and writing short stories and novels in my spare time. Violating all the traditions of small-town writers-to-be, I was never frenzied with impatience to be away or to experience life as it *truly* was in the city. Not then but later I understood that this was not so much a positive choice as a natural timidity, otherwise known as my naked fear of the tumultuous unknown of the big city. Whenever I thought *city* I dwelt only on a disastrous trip Mother and Joe and I made to the New York World's Fair in 1940. It was a weekend of frayed nerves, exhaustion, quarrels, tears, jostling crowds, rudeness, indifference, and waitings-in-line. Although I got to see Eleanor Holm's Aquacade and to hear Harry James and his new band, my conclusion was that I could live quite well without tackling New York City again and its gritty, hurrying chaos. I'd have missed a great adventure, but I didn't know that then.

And I'd never felt moved to complain about Hammondsport's provincialism or close-mindedness because it was true that the village was unusually cosmopolitan. I don't see how it could have been otherwise, since its output included champagne and airplanes. And I'd already discovered that through reading and correspondence you could bring the larger world about as close as you wanted it. Then, too, the lake and the wine kept drawing the world or a few of its celebrities to Hammondsport. One of the town legends is that Hoagy Carmichael wrote "Star Dust" while drifting along Keuka Lake in a canoe. Actually my impression is that Carmichael wrote "Star Dust" in about as many places as George Washington slept. What was indubitable was that Franklin Delano Roosevelt paused at Keuka once while he was on the campaign trail for president the first time. (An aunt of mine waded fully clothed and wearing a picture hat into Lake Keuka on that occasion as a gesture of total support for his candidacy.)

When I started my second year of high school in September of 1941 there was little doubt in my mind that Hammondsport and I were partners forever. The one large uncertainty was in the news. I was fifteen on that December seventh when the Japanese attacked Pearl Harbor. Despite the cocky assurances of the guys at the gas station that it would take no time at all to put Japan in its place, I couldn't quite believe it. I read the newspapers and *Time* carefully and I felt it was entirely possible that the war would go on long enough to see me into uniform. Yet I told myself that military service, like college, would mean only a temporary absence from Hammondsport. That was assuming I survived the war, which I didn't really think about until I enlisted two years later, but by then all my certainties had collapsed.

As the school year began I still clung to Hammondsport as my past, present, and future rolled into one. The family roots simply went too deep, I told myself, and I clung to them with a precocious and not entirely healthy pride and reassurance. To change the image I suppose I was making the past a kind of antiquarian security blanket. The roots gave a feeling of continu-

207

ity—my own included—and I was grateful for that intangible sense of security they provided.

Despite my parents' divorce and my father's death, I had no doubt that Uncle Charlie, who then led the winery, would have been pleased for me to come in and start learning the business. He had no son and his daughter Caroline was married to a successful Rochester lawyer and had her own life. (A few years later, when I wrote Uncle Charlie that I was going to work for a magazine, he wished me well, expressed regrets that I wouldn't be at PV, and remarked philosophically, "Journalists do seem wedded to their work.") But when I was fifteen I could still daydream about myself, now as a kindly, elderly figure, strolling amongst the dark and winey catacombs carved from the hillsides back in Jules Masson's time, and dreaming up plots.

But fantasies have a way of crumbling in the face of reality, and early in 1942 my mother announced that she was thinking about marrying again. I was absolutely astonished. Not fearful, jealous, angry, or any of the other negative emotions. I was in fact delighted, because you didn't have to be a genius to know that her life was not wonderful and had had no real prospects of getting better. But I was surprised out of my shoes. My father had been dead for four years and there was no longer any theological reason she could not marry again, but such a possibility had somehow never occurred to me or to Joe. We hadn't even had a clue that any courtship had been in progress. I couldn't recall that she had gone out to dinner on what might count as a date. (I just hadn't been paying attention, obviously.) In a lovely and gentle way she presented the possibility of marriage to us not as a *fait accompli* but as a request for permission from Joe, who was then not quite twelve, and me, who was about to be sixteen. I'm not sure what would have happened if we had opposed the idea, but our answers were never in doubt.

We knew him. He was a shy and serious man, but with an affirmative and appreciative laugh and an endless curiosity about almost everything on earth. His name was Charles Haynes and he was to have a considerable influence, all of it positive, on all our lives. He and our mother had met when he boarded in Hammondsport while working on a public works bridge project in the mid-thirties. He was a college graduate who had attended Harvard Business School, but this was the Depression. He had a lifelong abhorrence of debt and obligation and was doing essentially manual labor to stay solvent. When the economy improved he started his own firm, selling construction supplies, and he came through Hammondsport often. He was also an inveterate sender of newspaper clippings he thought would interest Mother or us. We received books and recipes and items of intelligence about the worlds of politics, business, and literature, all of which he found engrossing. I assumed, when Mother broke the news, that the courtship had been largely by mail and had been mostly about ideas. Later I realized how naive I was not to understand that romance afflicts adults, too, and that I had self-centeredly ignored a lovely courtship taking place before my very eyes.

After the delight, my not-very-delayed second realization (amid horror and panic) was that the marriage meant we would be moving away from Hammondsport. The unavoidable fact was that Charlie Haynes lived in the small family farmhouse in which he had been born on the north shore of Oneida Lake just east of the village of Cleveland (population five hundred). It was only about one hundred thirty miles northeast of Hammondsport, but in wartime 1942 it could as well have been on the far side of the moon. His father, whom he had looked after for years, had lately died, freeing my stepfather-to-be to marry for the first time. Mother was forty-four; he was thirty-eight.

I was stunned and scared at the prospect of leaving, and the prospect must have been only a little less earth-shaking for Mother; her own roots went very deep in the village. But I sensed soon enough that it was for her like being reborn—away from all the family and community pressures and away from all the painful memories. For Joe it meant leaving the B&H Railroad,

209

which he was still riding every Saturday. For me, it meant severing myself from all that colorful and comforting family history and starting all over again from scratch, leaving behind the friends of a lifetime, including a romance I was taking more seriously than the girl. I was abandoning the village that seemed as much a part of me as I was of it.

From the perspective of four decades it is obvious that the wrenching-away was the best thing that could have happened to all of us. It proved to be an endearing and fruitful marriage, which lasted twenty-three years until my mother died at the age of sixty-seven. To everyone's surprise, including her own, she produced a lovely daughter, named Nancy for her grandmother, at the age of forty-five.

Without the move from Hammondsport to the North Shore of Oneida Lake, I would almost certainly not have gone to Harvard—which I did at my stepfather's urging—and might or might not have found my way to the only career I ever truly hoped for, which was to earn my keep as a writer. Brother Joe would, I feel strongly, have found his way to the priesthood in any circumstances, but several aspects of our lives in Cleveland, including the influence of the local pastor who became his mentor, made his decision even more sure and serene than it might otherwise have been.

But ail that is hindsight talking. As I turned sixteen I was convinced my world had collapsed and I was to become a stateless wanderer, less than tragic but touched with sadness. (The pains of leaving were very real but the alarms for the future were grossly exaggerated.) Coincidentally the Charles Youngloves, who owned the house at 51 Lake Street which we had rented for all the years I can remember, now needed the house for their daughter and son-in-law, who had been displaced to Hammondsport from New Jersey by the war. We moved out, shipping the furniture to Cleveland and going to live temporarily with grandmother Nano Masson over on Vine Street. My collection of match folders did not survive the move, which was no loss, but my precious collection of pulp magazines also disappeared.

Mother became Mrs. Charles Haynes on June 1, 1942 at St. Gabriel's in Hammondsport and as best man I gave her away. The new Hayneses went off to Cleveland to set up housekeeping and Joe and I stayed on at my grandmother's. Mother came back to Hammondsport briefly, when I had a prearranged non-emergency appendectomy. After the operation, Mother took Joe to Cleveland and I stayed at Vine Street to recover. I spent the summer reading and chatting with old friends (in a rather terminal way, as if I were going into exile or so I remember it now). Almost nightly I walked two or three miles up a vineyard road to talk with the girl I was leaving behind. We sat on her lawn under the stars in the warm summer nights and our conversations were long and sad and philosophical, although I don't remember a word of them. It would be after midnight when I walked back down the vineyard road, serenaded by an occasional owl. My grandmother was very tolerant and trusting, as she had every right to be; it was an innocent time. After our last evening, I didn't see the girl again for nearly forty years.

On my last days in Hammondsport I made it a point to walk every street in the village, soaking up memories against what I could only foresee, very dramatically, as the long winter of the rest of my life. There were great experiences coming, but my overwhelming and self-pitying sense of loss blinded me to the possibilities that lay ahead.

When I wasn't walking around town I practiced driving my grandmother's Buick back and forth in her driveway. It was the only driving I had ever done and most times I could back up without veering into the hedge which grew along one side of the gravel.

Then on a day in late July of 1942, my grandmother and I set out to drive to Cleveland. Once we got out of town my grandmother insisted I take the wheel. I think she presumed I had had more driving experience than I had. Despite having to cope with the stick shift, I did quite nicely until I came to a stoplight on a slight rise on the main street in Geneva. I stalled a couple of times, but my grandmother waited calmly while I got the hang of it. Later I figured out how wise she was, offering me the chance to drive and thus distracting me from my long, long thoughts about saying goodbye to Hammondsport.

It worked. I made it through the stoplight and we sailed effortlessly through the rest of Geneva and on north, away from Hammondsport and into my new and unrooted life.

References

Baker, Frank. *Baker Ancestry: The Ancestry of Sam Baker, of Pleasant Valley, Steuben County, New York, with Some of His Descendants.* Compiled by Frank Baker. Chicago, 1914. Privately printed.

Clayton, W. W. *History of Steuben County, New York.* Philadelphia: Lewis, Peck & Co., 1879.

Isherwood, Christopher. *Down There on a Visit.* New York: Simon & Schuster, 1962.

O'Brien, Sharon, ed. *Willa Cather: Early Novels and Stories.* New York: The Library of America, 1987.

Swarthout, Laura L. *A History of Hammondsport to 1962.* Corning-Painted Post Historical Society, n.d.

BACK THERE WHERE THE PAST WAS

was composed in 11 on 13 Sabon on a Mergenthaler Linotron 202
by Partners Composition;
printed by sheet-fed offset on 50-pound, acid-free Glatfelter Natural Hi Bulk,
Smyth-sewn and bound over binder's boards in Holliston Roxite B,
with dust jackets printed in 2 colors,
by Braun-Brumfield, Inc.;
designed by Mary Peterson Moore;
and published by

SYRACUSE UNIVERSITY PRESS
SYRACUSE, NEW YORK 13244-5160